SOBRIETY
AMEN

Growth Beyond
The Initial
Spiritual Experience

John M. Nowak

Providence Two
Chino Valley, Arizona

Library of Congress Catalog Card Number: 98-92022

ISBN: 0-9666037-0-2

Printed by: Data Reproductions Corporation

Published by:
Providence Two
P.O. Box 2211
Chino Valley, AZ 86323
520-636-1120

Scripture quotations are from the King James Version of the Bible.

CONTENTS

Preface vi
Acknowledgments vii
Introduction viii

CHAPTER ONE – BEFORE

Seeking 10
Panic 15
Qualification 21
Materialism 36
Like Father, Like Son 39

CHAPTER TWO – AWARENESS

Religious vs. Spiritual 46
Forty Years in the Desert 53
God Talks to Us 56
Twelve Steps Toward Liberty 64
Emotional Stress and Spiritual Battles 69
God's Eternal Plan for You 76

CHAPTER THREE – ADVENTURE BEGINS

Just Keep Walking 86
I Threw the Horse 90
Physical Therapy 93
Sodom and Gomorrah 95
A New Kind of Desert 99
The Rosicrucian 101
He Knows Before We Ask 104
Bye-Bye, Bursitis 106
He is Able 112
Pentecost Sunday 116
A Fiery Exchange 124

CHAPTER FOUR – WINNERS ONLY

New Adventure – New Life   132
Solution to All Problems   142
Divine Healing   148
Cannibalism   155
Emotionalism   157
Why Do Some Things Happen?   160
Giving Up Things and Becoming Good First   164
Liberty in Christ   166
Repentance   170
Appropriating From God   178
Fruit of the Spirit   193
Commitment Unto Perfection   201

CHAPTER FIVE – CHALLENGE

Why A Saviour?   212
Continued Rebellion   216
Renewing of the Mind   226
Plan of Salvation   239
Senior Salvation   246
Challenge   250

Appendix   255
Bibliography   259

DEDICATION

"For ye are bought
with a price:
therefore glorify God
in your body,
and in your spirit,
which are God's."[1]

In following the Christ,
to witness unto Jesus
of repentance and remission of sins,
carrying the Word of God...
by His Spirit...
to others who have begun the walk.

PREFACE

*"Thou hast enlarged my steps under me
so that my feet did not slip."* [2]

Truly, My Higher Power has enlarged my steps. He has kept me from alcohol and other evil "spirits." He has been faithful to guide me along precarious paths during years filled with turmoil, as I sought His direction and spiritual growth. He has enlarged my coast.

This book is part of my story: where I was and, by the grace of God, where I am going. It is my endeavor to share, carry the message, seek God's will and carry that out. The book tells of my spiritual awakening and some of the continuing adventure since. I don't pretend to be a theologian or great student of the Bible; I just want to share the love of God that works in my life. By sharing my experiences, I trust God to inspire others to walk with Him toward a fullness, all for their blessing and for His glory.

In the Alcoholics Anonymous Program, I was taught to be sure I had something to give before I tried to give it to others. As a Christian, I am sure I have something to give, something to share, at any phase of my growth.

This book can be beneficial to those who have accepted the challenge of spiritual progress or those who need to know some keys for opening the door to spiritual progress. Once they walk through that door, they are on the way to a knowledge of resolution for their problems and perfection, as it can be on Earth and as it can be eternally.

ACKNOWLEDGEMENTS

My greatest acknowledgment is to God for the liberties in Christ and for the blessings of Alcoholics Anonymous, which He has steadfastly protected and sustained for the benefit of so many.

Gratitude is expressed to those in Alcoholics Anonymous who persistently follow God's will in faithful support of each person's quest for a spiritual experience.

A special thank you and gratitude to one of the ladies in our church congregation who, years ago, reconstructed the manuscript from the copies that survived the "Fiery Exchange." I don't remember her name but wish to thank her in this book, hoping we will meet again in our earthly adventure.

Especial thanks to my beautiful Christian wife Judith Ann for putting the manuscript on the computer, and for the patient support she has given me during its development.

INTRODUCTION

For so many, what they call religion is and has always been the total sum of a relationship with God. A lifetime is spent, for the majority, in the religious state without the reality of God experiences, a spiritual awakening leading to tangible moves of God in life.

Although one cannot realize spirituality through the events in the life of another, it is possible for the true seeker to find spiritual reality by learning about those incidents and how God brings them about.

It is true that God works differently in each life because we have a special purpose in the very personal adventure He has created for each of us. However, God never changes, and He is always lovingly open to any sincere soul.

My intention in writing this book is to share the movement of God in my life, His teaching process behind it and encouragement of others to move from a religious state to one of true spirituality. As well, it is a process which continues into eternity with every hope for the here and now.

My experiences impress me to believe that, simply, a sincere initial repentance brings a true spiritual experience and a God-seeking heart, in place of a self-directed life, which will bring anyone to personal knowledge of the one and only true living God.

Chapter One

Before

*"I am come that they might have life,
and they might have it more abundantly."* [3]

SEEKING

People who have a God-reality experience, can have a successful life of continual spiritual growth through Jesus Christ, on continually higher levels.

This book tells how an initially repentant spiritual beginning can grow into an exciting God-dependent fullness in Christ.

For those of you who have completed a thorough self-inventory with amendments, this book is intended to help you realize the work God has done in your life, to inspire you to higher levels, and to show you how this can be accomplished. One of the reasons a person can proceed to higher spiritual levels, beyond normal comprehension, is because he has reached a point of helplessness in "self." When this point is reached a person becomes more willing to accept what is right. Honesty goes hand in hand with growth as God removes your bonds and prepares you for submission to His will. Then God can work in your life and keep you in dependency on Him alone.

For others, this book is intended to help form a new attitude toward repentance, which will produce benefits resulting in a very tangible experience with God.

Through the Holy Bible (The Word of God), you can find life's purpose and become free of all worldly bondage by the fulfillment of His plan for your life and through spiritual growth.

"If ye continue in my word, then ye are my disciples indeed:
And ye shall know the truth and the truth shall make you free." [4]

I encourage you to put your complete trust in God, let Him manifest Himself to you, and place you in the wonderful adventure He has for your life.

Submitted for the work of God's will in your life, you are on the brink of moving to inexhaustible heights. If you have honestly asked God for knowledge of His will and the power to carry that out, expect Him to reveal himself to you—Persist!

In my case, I sought God and it was my desire to know His mind. It was also God's plan, as it is for all people. I prayed many hours and agonized before Him. Then I found myself being further involved in seeking His true concept and attending to His will.

Eventually I was moved from one location to another and discovered that my eyes were more and more on Him and that He was keeping me. I realized I was no longer fighting thoughts of drinking. As I sought God and prayed, I was moved into the realm of His wonderful plan for me.

If you are one who is seeking the next step after hitting the bottom of life, read on! May God inspire you to be more concerned with His will, and manifest miracles in your life that make Him real to you, personally.

You will see in the later pages how God proceeded to establish me in the Word, establish Himself within my heart and life, and how my subsequent experiences with Christ affected my life.

Self-inventory and repentance concern spiritual deliverance through the Word of God and through the sharing of it with others.

Many of us tried religion for deliverance instead of Jesus and failed. Man-made religion is one thing, Jesus is another! Not knowing this, many turn away from Him as well as religion. This is the crucial point that makes all the difference, which you will see as you continue to read. Also, many will be looking for an easy way out, bypassing the necessary repentance inventory as commanded by God.

Alcoholics Anonymous (A.A.) has been triumphant for years in helping people live sober lives and helping them take part in a church. Even man-made religion and A.A. is better than a life of drunkenness. However, a Christ experience is the beginning of the ultimate for all.

The Holy Spirit of God has been drawing many to a fullness in Jesus Christ, and one needs to know that the Bible is the foundation for that fullness.

There is a certain element who do not attain because they are discouraged by the thought of the drabness of a spiritual existence. May they see that spirituality is not just going to church and sitting on a pew.

There is more! If your experience (religious or spiritual) has begun to grow dull, there is hope! Pray, and let God put His Spirit in your heart. You will experience a new exciting adventure, which will last for the rest of your days.

"But they that seek the Lord shall not want any good thing." [5]

I cried out to the Lord.

"This poor man cried, and the Lord heard him,
and saved him out of all his troubles." [6]

How merciful and forgiving He is, just as His Word says. I continuously prayed for His true concept until He began to work in my life. Upon turning things over to God, He started me on the road to salvation and freedom from fears and other bondages.

I didn't even know what I had or what was happening to me except that I felt a new life surging through me. The question came to me, "How many others are on the brink of a new adventure, but do not realize how they got there or how to move ahead?" I pray that this will be your time.

In this book I relate some of my experiences prior to my time in A.A. Successive events, which followed progressively, agreed with the teachings of the A.A. Program in regard to its being a lifetime spiritual school. This book goes beyond the teachings of the Program in that it shows continuation beyond life here on Earth, as we know it—a life that extends into eternity. It is the story of how God took my life and is teaching me day by day. It is a graduation of a babe from liquids to solids.... from milk to meat.

I look back upon the Program and recall the feelings and expressions, evident in Christianity, as I had never seen them before. I called it Christianity, because it was the best name I knew for it. The Program is not taught as Christianity, but rather reference is made only to "God."

Since A.A. does not recognize any specific spiritual group, the name of Jesus is not used in A.A. The only time I heard anyone speak of Jesus in the Program was when a man in Ft. Worth, Texas, concluded his lead, "...and I call my God, Jesus Christ."

The primary A.A. principles are all based on the Bible.

All things were made by God, and Jesus came to provide abundance in the use of these things. A.A. is one of those special instruments that God has provided so that people may come to the fullness of Jesus Christ.

*"I came that they might have life,
and that they might have it more abundantly."* [7]

I feel, as do most alcoholics in A.A., that if all people were exposed to some time in the Program, the world would be a much better place in which to live. A.A. is a program of true initial repentance, which is the basic Christian foundation, but one that is often not built upon.

I give all the glory to Jesus Christ for my salvation, including my deliverance from alcoholism. And I consider A.A. as a tremendous gift, from God.

My intent is to share what the Lord has given me a day at a time, so that others might realize the potential in their future. I pray that they might step out and have the abundance that God meant for all to have, until that final graduation when Christ reaches out to take us home.... a perfect gem!

PANIC

It seems imperative that I lay some groundwork on my past regarding an occurrence of my childhood that greatly influenced my subsequent years. Also, when it is kept in mind as the reader goes on, it will enhance the appreciation of the greatness of God and the wonderful move that He has made upon my life, for His glory.

Born in 1929, my childhood, until the age of twelve, was spent in a coal mining town in Pennsylvania. My Father, a mild-mannered man from a family of eight children, was a coal miner for more than twenty-five years. My Mother was one of three girls who were orphaned at an early age and grew up with a grave element of insecurity and fear. I was the third of three boys, one to three years apart, until my kid brother came along twelve years later. Being the "baby" for twelve years, I inherited many fears from my Mother, who was overly protective and overbearing, which, I learned, are two areas common in most alcoholic backgrounds.

The occurrence took place in my sixth-grade schoolroom; I was twelve. It seems that a great excitement hit me. I felt tremendous fear, blood rushed to my head, I shook all over, my heart pounded furiously, and I can't recall just what else. I jumped up from my seat, rushed to the teacher, crying and in great confusion and fear of what was happening. The teacher held me in her arms until I calmed some; then she got in touch with my parents. Although she didn't know exactly what the condition was, she was familiar with it because she had a nephew who had been similarly afflicted.

My parents took me to several doctors, but none knew just what was wrong, and we were told that I would outgrow the condition.

The attacks continued chronically until my parents took me out of school for a year. Life was nothing but a continuous saga of fear, fear, fear. I would run to my mother in a panic, and she would hold me until the fear subsided and I was able to return to play, if I dared even to leave her side.

By now some of you have guessed that this condition is what is called a panic, or anxiety attack. In years gone by, no one knew what caused this; consequently I lived many years with this fearsome condition undiagnosed.

For those who are not familiar with panic attacks, let me insert an article here that I wrote for a writing class in 1996, which tries to capture some of the emotion involved.

Fear and Panic

Every faculty of your mind is preoccupied with a threat.

Hopelessness prevails because there is no way out.

Anxiety keeps tearing at your every fiber, waiting for the unknown terror to strike.

Your total body system is racing; heart and lungs are frantically overworking.

Your nerves tell you that you can't stand anymore turmoil.

You are desperate for a good ending to the situation, yet you 'know' that it's going to be a bad one, and maybe the final one—death or insanity.

Uncertainty about everything reigns as heavy, black smoke over a blazing pit of hell.

If it is an ongoing situation, there is withdrawal and isolation from others.

In time you become introverted and feel a sense of inferiority.

Self-consciousness sets in because you are sure people can see that you are nervous, and they can see it and comment on it.

In the midst of the panic, you desperately keep crying out with all your being, "God, please help me."

You die a thousand deaths a day and awaken in horror in the night, with your heart pounding and sweat soaking your body.

Sleep comes only as a surrender to mental fatigue.

You often choke on the medication taken to calm you, and it doesn't seem to do any good. "Maybe it's just sugar water. No, the doctor wouldn't try to trick me."

Depression hits so hard that you seem to be out of your body and out of reality, and it's extremely difficult to concentrate on anything but fear.

On the brightest of sunny days, you are convinced that it's dark and cloudy outside until you go to a window, look out and confirm the sunshine. When you turn away from the window, you return to the immediate darkness.

Your mind races at an amazing rate: What's going to happen to me? What's going to happen to my family? Will I suffer this for 50 years? 60? 70? 80? When will it end? Will it make me commit suicide? Oh, God, please, please help me.

As I write this section of the book, I weep uncontrollably because it is such an emotional realization that Jesus has kept me all these years through every kind of dilemma, trial, and separation from the "normal" life. My weeping turns into a burst of prayer in tongues because He has been faithful to never leave me or forsake me. His faithful grace has enabled me to overcome many impossible situations. He has elevated me to greater security in Him by freeing me from bondage, as He has brought me out.

As time went on, there was relief, but life remained full of stress and anxiety, and the condition persisted. I was able to maintain some semblance of a normal life and go on to a profitable, exciting, and interesting career in aerospace as a design engineer. But always in the backdrop was the mystery of the panic attack condition. Yes, I did outgrow some of it but the real progress came when I began to use the Word of God to combat the illness.

> *"For God hath not given us the spirit of fear; but of power, and of love, and of a sound mind."* [8]

This Scripture was my mainstay for years, repeated many times in a given day. I repeated it over and over as an affirmation until I felt calm. I also used it as a deterrent to fear when feeling nervous. The energy of fear was turned into the spiritual energy that overcame fear, spiritual laziness, and spiritual ignorance.

Sometime in the early 70s in New Orleans, I attended a prayer meeting in a private residence. Our opening session was a time of confession and prayer. Two men, who had come to minister, moved about the circle, praying for each individual as he or she confessed. They began praying for me. During the prayer, one of them reached out, touched me on the forehead and said, "And I rebuke that nervous condition in the name of Jesus." I had never seen these men before, don't know who they were and have never seen them since. The anxiety/panic attack condition was revealed to them by the Holy Spirit of God and that day was reduced to approximately fifty percent of its ferocity.

I was single, seeking the Lord with all my heart, participating in the witnessing of Jesus in funeral homes, hospitals, prisons and wherever I was prompted to go. God had already given me determination by the power of the Holy Spirit to be a disciple, even in the throes of my ongoing panic attacks. God was teaching me to be content in the knowledge that His strength was more effective in my weakness.

As time went on, I continued to fight the panic-attack battle with the Word. There were times when I would lower my head, close my eyes, clench my fists, rebuke the Devil and plead the blood of Jesus against him until peace and serenity came. I know that the gifts and reality of God demonstrated in the Bible's Book of Acts are just as viable today as ever. Unfortunately people often seek His gifts for personal glory instead of seeking and praising the Lord, and allowing Him to bless them in His way and time.

Eventually the panic attacks came under control by use of the Word. The Holy Spirit is capable of making us strong and healing us by renewing our minds in spiritual combat when we read, study, and make His Word a part of our inner being. It is not necessarily the memorization of all Scripture, but by His making the Word's intent a working part of our psyche. The miracle working Word of the Holy Bible replaces the destructive, negative elements of Satan.

Just a few years ago, my wife Judith handed me a newspaper and asked me to look at an article she had been reading. She said, "Look at this. It sounds like the condition you have described." Sure enough, the article described the same type of panic attacks that had been undefined for the prior fifty years.

I'm so glad we have a God who cares and knows more than anyone about anything. There was a time after going to doctors when I got on my knees and said, "Lord, if I am to be healed, you will be the one to do it." I have nothing against going to a doctor. Some of them are the finest of people, but Jesus has all knowledge and is the greatest healer of all time.

QUALIFICATION

The term "qualification" in Alcoholics Anonymous means to give a general, personal testimonial of one's rudiments with respect to life as an active alcoholic. The purpose of qualification in the A.A. Program continues to become clearer to me, as well as its significance in my progress and growth as a Christian. Qualification was a part of my confession and repentance, in obedience to God.

Qualification, enables other alcoholics to know that I have "been there." My qualification illustrates some of the fire that I have gone through, in which the preliminary steps of learning were taken.

This is my qualification:

My name is John and I am an alcoholic. I took the statistical route of 18 years to reach the point of no return. My drinking "career" began at the age of eighteen in 1947. My first serious drinking experience was with boilermakers (whisky and beer) and it pretty much remained boilermakers for me for the duration. My drinking began in a small steel town named Blawnox, Pennsylvania, which is situated along the Allegheny River just north of Pittsburgh, Pennsylvania, and it ended in 1968 in Columbus, Ohio, when I was thirty-eight. The last seven years of drinking were pretty much a hell for me, as well as for everyone else in my life.

It is difficult to remember, but it seems as though my drinking amplified to gross proportions in the late 50s. I usually worked hard at whatever I did and was a "self-made" man, which, along with my self-righteousness, gave me adequate justification for my drinking. I always made good money and sometimes wonder if that was a blessing or a curse, because I was able to drink all I wanted. It was my time to concentrate on material things; I started out appreciating them and ended up not appreciating them.

The early stages of my drinking were somewhat of a social thing. In later years it became more solitary. I usually preferred to drink alone and had a large capacity for drink. Many people didn't know I drank and that was the way I wanted it. In the later stages of drinking I knew that most people knew, and I also knew I was kidding myself that they didn't. It really didn't matter whether others knew or not; the important thing was that I could rationalize, excuse myself within, and keep on drinking.

The following is one of the more exciting adventures of those hangover days:

It was a typical, gray Saturday morning in fall as I drove to Northway Airport in Columbus, Ohio, where I had been taking private pilot training. The usual shakes and morning nausea prevailed as I forced myself to continue puffing on my cigar, for whatever I was getting out of it. I turned the big, old, black Chrysler off Morse Road into the parking lot and stepped out to meet my flight instructor.

I knew the time for my solo flight was near and I was terrified that I might have to take it in my hung-over condition. A grand drinking spree the night before is not the recommended procedure prior to one's solo flight. It didn't take long to find out that this was the day for my solo, because we proceeded to do simulated emergency landings and other pre-solo work.

Eventually, we landed and taxied near the take-off point at the end of the runway. By this time, I had made several overtures about not feeling too good and mumbled something about having a party the night before. My instructor had been a Navy flight instructor for some 3,400 hours and wasn't much impressed except to say, "You're making me nervous – I'm getting out of here. You take it up and stay up as long as you want." As it turned out, I shot five takeoffs and landings, flew a total of 50 minutes.... and lived.

My second solo flight, which took place three weeks later, was not quite the same. I flew for 2 hours and 20 minutes, doing takeoffs, landings, steep and shallow turns and power-off stalls. (At this particular time, spins were not part of the required student instruction).

At the stall point of one of my power-off stalls, I remembered that my instructor had advised me that, in order to prevent engine stall, it was important during air work, not to let the engine rpm get too low. Noting that the rpm was low, I quickly reached forward and grabbed the throttle at the panel center. In so doing, I used the left rudder for a leverage point. Since the plane had reached a point of stall, left rudder and a little throttle was all it needed to whip over into a spin. My eyes crossed and nothing was discernible; I was unable to set a flight directional reference. However, the rate at which everything was spinning past the windshield let me know pretty quickly that I had gotten myself into "a spin." I lowered my head and looked at the floor to re-focus my eyes. When I looked down, I saw that I had the left rudder hard against the floor. I didn't waste much time trying to figure out why I had done such a thing, but immediately neutralized the rudder position then waited to see what would come next.

My mind was working overtime wondering if this was my day to die. (I couldn't spend much time on that thought either).

Things I had read about spins began to run through my mind. The idea of neutralizing all the controls and waiting for the plane to right itself held no appeal for me whatsoever. I had to do something, quick! I neutralized all controls and tried pulling back on the wheel, but the plane continued to spin. The wheel was as firm as a pancake in my hands. So I waited, shook, sweated and continued to spin. Having depleted my available knowledge on spins, I decided to try the wheel again. This time it felt somewhat firm, so I pulled it all the way back. The plane came out of the spin so rapidly that I felt as if I was going to be pushed through the bottom of the seat.

After taking a few moments to pull myself together, I decided I had to do a few more stalls right then or I would never have the courage to fly again. I was very much frightened, but pride wouldn't let me call it a day until I was satisfied that I had conquered the fear. Though I performed a few more stalls, it was six weeks before I tried it again. I was happy to put the Taylorcraft N96091 into the hanger that day and get to the nearest drink.

This experience was typical of the way I was "enjoying" life in September of 1957.

As I look back, I received confirmation as to the way God had chosen me to walk with Him, but I didn't realize it until eleven years later:

"If I take the wings of the morning...Even there shall thy hand lead me, and thy right hand shall hold me." [9]

This was just one of the many times I could have died without knowing Him. It makes me have a greater appreciation of His love for all of us. The sad part is that then I was ignorant of the wonderful plan He had for me.

As time went by, a lot of time and energy were wasted through drinking. But there were always signs of ambition, such as when I would make home improvements.

My home situation, however, degenerated to such a degree that I wanted to spend very little time there. A lot of time was spent in bars, and rather than going home, I would drive into the country. I know, like all alcoholics, that much time was spent behind the wheel, and doing other things, which endangered my life and the lives of others. But I know now that God had His hand on me and brought me through all of that for a purpose. As we said in the Program, "The Lord protects innocent children and drunks."

My experience in the drinking years included an arrest for intoxication, running red lights, speeding and reckless operation.

"Be not deceived; God is not mocked:
for whatsoever a man soweth, that shall he also reap." [10]

I had sown a long time and when I began to reap, the bulk of the trouble came in my home situation.

I look back and remember those days when I sat in a bar drinking solitarily, and a little voice in the background would say, "You've gone too far and you are really going to pay for it." I thought it was too late, but I didn't know what was ahead. I really didn't have the capacity to do much of anything except to survive as best I could—just to go on living and wait to see what was going to happen, even though I felt that eventually my life would end in insanity or death.

In those hours of solitary drinking, alcohol had also given me a deceptive lift. I used to think of how I was going to come out on top and how I was going to "show the world." I spent many hours building myself up, but then the next morning, I would find myself on the bottom again, going nowhere.

During part of my drinking years, I frequented a particular tavern. On one occasion, as I was about to enter this tavern, a man stepped in front of me and said, "Young man, are you a Christian?" I looked at him and mumbled yes as I brushed past him. Though only a few words had passed between us, I was touched by the incident. If I had asked myself the same question, I could have drunk just as I usually did without feeling any conviction. The fact that another person asked the question shocked me into a new awareness. With the religious background I had, I felt that I was a Christian, but this incident made me feel cheap and made me realize that I was certainly far from God's will.

Bar drinking was only a part of it. I also drank at home, during the time I could bear to be there, and much of that was usually after everyone was tucked in for the night. Some nights I had been to the bar and absorbed my store of hard liquor, but many times it was not enough to take me to the level I wanted, so I had to make another run or two. I had to go back and get reinforced so I could sit at home with a beer and sustain the glow until I drank myself into unconsciousness.

I was afraid to drink anymore because I knew it was too late in the day to be drinking. I was afraid not to drink anymore because it just seemed I had to keep going until I was unconscious. Yet I fought sleep to drink. I just kept craving more.

I know what it is like to have my life so centered around alcohol that everything is planned around it. Seldom was there a day spent in the country when I didn't make provisions, either having alcohol in the trunk of the car so I could get to it when I wanted it, or making sure that I could get back home soon enough to keep the glow going.

Sometimes during camping trips I would tour the local area to learn where the bars and booze supply were. It was not uncommon for me to leave the campsite and drive miles after everyone was asleep so I could buy alcohol. I usually picked an A-1 state park campsite, where there was adequate protection for the family, so that I could slip away at night and drink feeling that they were safe.

I began taking Librium, using it only sparingly in the mornings. I was trying to maintain some semblance of emotional stability that would enable me to get through the day, so that I could return to drinking again at night.

It seems as if I went through this cycle thousands of times: driving to work in the morning—sick, nervous, praying, begging God, "Lord, please help me to get through this day and I will never drink again. I won't drink anymore." I had dizzy spells and the shakes. I used large amounts of shaving lotion, chewed gum, and often kept a cigar in my mouth to keep the smell of alcohol away from other people. My mind raced a mile a minute with all this conflict inside, while I tried to get a job done. Sometimes the Librium helped. Other times it added to my discomfort and made me sicker and more nervous.

In the afternoon, usually around two or three o'clock, the rough edges would start to wear off. I'd begin to feel a little more comfortable and, in the back of my mind, would start planning my next drunk. By the time the quitting beeper sounded at work, I was in pretty good shape.... I had made it through another working day.

Generally, I made it home, had dinner and stayed around long enough to fulfill my obligations as meagerly as I could. I would get involved in some little task in the garage or workshop so that I could make myself feel useful. I got a little time delay so I could slip away without being quite so noticed, like a little boy who slips away from home when no one is looking, and once he gets around the corner, he is safe!

Sometimes my drinking sprees would go on until the wee hours of the morning. Other times they would continue for only a short time at a bar but with enormous consumption. Then I'd go home with a supply of beer to keep it going, while working in the workshop or sitting in front of the TV so that I wouldn't look too stupid while I drank my life away.

I know well what it is like to wake up at six o'clock in the morning still heavily under the influence, thinking it might be one or two o'clock and thinking that I still had hours to sleep and sober up before it was time to go to work. Then a sudden fear would grasp me. I was afraid to look at the clock, knowing that it might be time to get up. It *was* time to get up! Then I had to furiously run the mental course again of how to get myself excused from work that day. What would I do? How could I do it? Perhaps I had just done it yesterday or the day before, or late last week. The walls were closing in as my panic increased. My affliction became a treacherous collar that was getting smaller and smaller. I hated to face the night. I remember waking up to respiratory spasms where I had only half of my normal breathing capacity. Satan had his hands tightly around my throat, trying to make each attack my ticket to hell.

I was afraid to see morning come realizing the shape I would be in. The mornings seemed to be growing closer and closer together.

"So am I made to possess months of vanity,
and wearisome nights are appointed to me.
When I lie down, I say,
When shall I arise, and the night be gone?
And I am full of tossings to and fro
unto the dawning of the day." [11]

Approximately two years before I reached bottom, I went to a few A.A. meetings. But then I decided I had not had enough yet. So I went back out for more.

Near the end of my drinking days, it took two days to sober up. Two days off work, in bed, literally sick, I was in no condition to walk let alone try to begin life again!

During the last few occurrences, I felt as if I was on the verge of delirium tremens (D.T.'s). I began to have horrible sensations and feelings. I felt as though I was on the verge of seeing monstrous things and having terrible things happen to me. My fear ran very high. Having lived such a negative existence, everything had deteriorated to where life seemed pretty fruitless and I had little hope left.

In A.A. I experienced the ability to stay sober for a month, weeks, or even five minutes at a time, by striving to live the Program—a day at a time.

"Sufficient unto the day is the evil thereof." [12]

Literally, I grasped a piece of furniture, workbench or whatever.... in last futile attempts to keep from moving toward the car and a bar.

I know the hell of having a drunk planned in the back of the mind, knowing without any doubt that I was going to be drunk.... when I really didn't want to be! It is a feeling of having very little control, or none at all, as if I was two people— One that is inside with the control, and the other, a zombie, an empty shell, forced to follow a preplanned route.

Finally, after seven months battling in A.A., and many domestic pressures, I was ready to take the subway out of darkness and dare to face the sunlight on the surface streets of life.

Many of these things and others I shared as I spoke in A.A. in succeeding months. The alcoholic life was a hideous experience that included things not fit to tell beyond the personal inventory I shared with God and only one other person. There is no need to place these things before my eyes anymore. God has forgiven me for all of them and I have learned to accept forgiveness in His gracious mercy.

"...forgetting those things which are behind,
and reaching forth unto those things which are before,
I press toward the mark for the prize of the high calling
of God in Christ Jesus." [13]

Then the celestial rains fell upon the raging forest fire, and raindrops of joy and hope began refreshing me within. Thank you, Jesus!

"...is not this a brand plucked out of the fire?" [14]

A new experience. Waking up in the morning, seeing a new day—sober. I was free of the alcoholic sting, nervousness, emotional and physical turmoil. It was a wonderful feeling to be alive, to be sober—something I had never thought I would feel again.

I know now that this was a little spark of God's love. This joy, even when it lasted a short period of time, was a wondrous new feeling. I began to trust God. I had cried out to God in all sincerity and when He knew I had had enough, He stretched out His hands and began to remold me. These meager feelings of joy, hope, and peace, only instantaneous in longevity, came closer together in time. Progressively, they stayed for longer periods as I shared with others who were in need.

This was a very trying interval when I was passing from a totally hopeless situation to a new life, a new liberty, a new existence. But then I could not really call it an existence anymore, because I knew *that* word applied to the years that had preceded. How gratifying it was just to walk down the street and be able to look people in the eye. I now knew how many had been passing me by, pretending not to see me. Even though I had a haunting background, it didn't matter because I was sober, and a broken life was better than death.

In the Program, I began to notice the glitter in people's eyes, until I became quite conscious of it. There was joy, peace—unlike anything I had ever felt before. I yearned within my heart for the day that I would look like that. I wanted to *feel* what I was seeing in their eyes.

Intermittently, there were treacherous battles going on inside, battles dealing with the negative elements, such as resentment. Evil things begin to build up as a person's mind is overwhelmed by sad impressions.

No one knows better than I, that the negative way is the way of the alcoholic. It is a life under barrage by the evil spirits of the universe.

This time of my life symbolized the dethroning of the evil spirits.

Not all people have the same crisis or difficulty, but there is not one who doesn't have trials in this life. The same rewards and blessings that I have received thus far, and the promises of the greater ones ahead for me, are the same ones available for everyone.

Eternal life after the earthly one is my hope, promise and belief.

This brings to mind an A.A. meeting I attended at Palos Verdes during an employment period in the Los Angeles area of California. The evening speaker related his feelings about death. In essence, he said that he looked upon death as a process wherein he moved from one room to another. I don't know what the man's spiritual affiliations were, but I can't help but think that if this man followed the A.A. principles to date and sought God diligently, that by now, the Lord has shown him the true eternal life. I pray that He has.

Although I was growing in A.A., receiving many blessings, I still had an unsatisfied feeling. There was a churning, yearning inside. It was quite comfortable compared to the preceding years but there was still something wanting.

I know that this was God continuing to work. This feeling continued for a couple of years after I had left the program. I have a similar feeling today, but this time I know what it is. The unsatisfied feeling then was the Spirit of God working to get me to recognize Him, to consciously accept Christ as my Saviour, to find the real way of life in His true concept.

Today, I have somewhat mixed feelings. I yearn, because I am still in my human form knowing that there is a greater adventure ahead with Jesus, where I will be for all eternity, free from all the problems, strife, difficulties and heartaches of the world.

I had a favorite daydream during times of revelation through the Word: To sit on the ground, at the feet of Jesus Christ…surrounded by little children…their love…and flowers…to hear the Word of the Holy Bible, taught by Him…revelation by revelation…just to eat the bread of life, share it with the little ones…and thank Him for Gethsemane…and Calvary. After the first thousand years, maybe a second thousand years….

"Thy words were found, and I did eat them;
and thy word was unto me the joy and rejoicing of mine heart:
I am called by thy name, O Lord God of hosts." [15]

On the other hand, there is a desire to stay because my new life has brought a new adventure. The adventure here is one of a quiet, peaceful fellowship that I want to enjoy in sharing His works in my life, an adventure that is free from so many of those earthly difficulties. It is a feeling of dependence on God and security in knowing that He takes care of me day by day. The excitement of what He is going to do next, when I am able to keep my self out of the way, and what new opportunities I will have to share with others, is what He has given me.

Having an experience with Christ and becoming a born-again Christian gives one internal assurance of eternal life. Christians with a real experience can't keep from telling what Jesus is doing in their lives. Yes, sometimes the "groaning" is still there, but it is gratifyingly different from the past unrest.

> *"For we know that the whole creation groaneth*
> *and travaileth together until now. And not only they,*
> *but ourselves also, which have the first fruits of the Spirit,*
> *even we ourselves groan within ourselves,*
> *waiting the adoption, to wit, the redemption of our body."* [16]

All people are included in God's plan.

> *"For the grace of God that bringeth salvation*
> *hath appeared to all men."* [17]

I promised before I started to write this book that I would be honest, and I have endeavored to put forth an honest picture of what it is like to be a Christian, by my own experience.

No matter the condition or difficulty you may be experiencing, this book can be used as a handbook to help you find God and make Him real in your life; to help you to embark on a completely new adventure in this world and discover an eternal life of love for Christ, Who makes it all possible. In this book, it is possible to find definite recommendations that can lead you to the start of a whole new life, with purpose and rewards—in Christ.

MATERIALISM

If we live for worldly, material things, this is all we can expect. How can we possibly hope for anything after death, when here only material things mean anything to us? If we stop to think about it, it is common sense to realize that if we take this matter seriously, we can change our whole life.

In the beginning, it is difficult for a person to think of something to hope for after death on Earth. It is difficult to imagine how the conviction of a Saviour and eternal life changes the perspective. The blessings are far beyond any material, temporary thing that can ever be attained on Earth.

Faith in eternal promises and the abundant life grows with regular reading of The Bible. God also gives faith and strength through miracles performed in one's life. He shows that He is real, confirming to one's heart that there is a life beyond earthly death. There *is* something to hope for.

"For we are saved by hope: but hope that is seen is not hope;
for what a man seeth, why doth he yet hope for?" [18]

In a material sense, the abundant life is comparable to having a new car and enjoying it with few mishaps and necessary maintenance along the way. The abundant life is fed or fueled by the Holy Bible. The Word works through the Holy Spirit. The opposite is like having a new automobile without gasoline and you're sitting on the porch looking at it. No mishaps, no maintenance, no enjoyment, no growth from travel—all because you have no fuel. One can be a Christian and yet be a porch-sitter without the Word. The more of the Word, the greater the life. The abundant life with all its power and gifts is not just for those other people in the churches; it is for everyone!

One of the things that is different in being a Christian is looking toward the last mile, that last hour on this Earth. If you are looking at it now and all you can feel is depression, uncertainty, fear, doubt, and unhappiness, you are living a life that is far below what almighty God has for you in His bountiful love and blessings, for this Earth and the new Earth.

If you are living the life of a Christian with a real experience, your eyes are on the Saviour, Jesus Christ. If He does not take you in the Rapture of the Church, with other Christians (which will be discussed later), He stands there as you draw your last breath, His hand extended, saying, "Come home." You know that in that moment, every person, every thing that has been in your life, that has meant anything to you, will be less significant.... for you will be seeing the One who made everything possible in your adventuresome life as a Christian. You will know that you have reached the point you have actually yearned for while in the valleys, on Earth.

On one occasion, I had a discussion with a man who was telling me about his closeness to God on a recent camping trip. He spoke of the natural beauty and, in his sincere way, was expressing what closeness to God meant to him. In our conversation, he expressed desire for my agreement. I related that I've had similar experiences and it is beautiful. It is a closeness to God because all these beautiful things that God created draw us near to Him. I explained how, in these situations, my relationship to God gains meaningfulness through the Scriptures.

He felt that perhaps Christians did nothing but read the Bible, whereupon I advised him that reading the Bible was just part of the blessings of God, which seem to start in a small way. The miracles seem to be pretty far apart. The working of God's hand in one's life doesn't seem to come very often in the beginning. But as time goes by, and one draws closer to God, the blessings become greater, the time intervals become shorter and the communication becomes more readily accessible. A greater amount of time in the Word benefits in greater faith, but any time in The Word reaps manifold blessings.

> *"So then faith cometh by hearing,*
> *and hearing by the Word of God."* [19]

Consider that new car or yacht, or any other material possessions you may have. Imagine the most extraordinary commodities you could hope to attain in this world and the resultant, though temporary, joy you receive from them. Those cannot be compared with what the Lord can give in terms of joy or security in times of need, when you are facing momentous oppression and adversity.

LIKE FATHER, LIKE SON

Before I began reading the Word, God was only a theory to me, not a reality.

I thought I believed in "The Lord's Prayer," but these were just words that I had learned in a religious environment. As a born-again Christian, I believe He is my Father, and I honor Him more than my earthly father.

It must be rather disconcerting for God to look upon Earth and see those who pray to "Our Father," then observe the scant attention paid to Him as they go about their busy lives in the world that He created for their pleasure and victorious adventure.

It might be similar to a relationship between parents and their grown children, wherein the children ignore them most of the week, approach them on Sunday for an hour or so, pay tribute to them and then leave for another week.

Children have their parents in their hearts. They go to them not only in times of difficulty and strife. They go to them many times every day because they love and want their love to be reciprocated because they desire security, comfort and assurance from their parental source. Just as they are parents to their children, just as they love them, just as they expect their children to come to them any hour of the day or night, our Heavenly Father looks for us to come to Him that He might bless us. Likewise we need Jesus in our hearts and as our intercessor in heaven.

If a Christian does not read the Bible, he doesn't have the faith or the relationship with God that he needs to live productively.

"Being born again, not of corruptible seed, but of incorruptible,
by the word of God, which liveth and abideth forever." [20]
"Whosoever transgresseth, and abideth not
in the doctrine of Christ, hath not God.
He that abideth in the doctrine of Christ,
he hath both the Father and the Son." [21]

An occasional visit to a church, or a plea to God when something goes wrong, can hardly establish fellowship with God in a Father-Son relationship.

This is another area in which it is different to be a Christian with a real experience. A Christian knows Christ in his heart. Many will not even mention the name of Jesus except in church circles or with others of the same religion.

A true experience makes one believe in Him. It gives one an opportunity and a boldness to witness to people because they sense a mysterious contentment in the Christian and want to know why. I wish I could say that I am always that kind of a Christian but then, I don't know anyone who is.

There have been days, weeks, even months at a time when my relationship with God has been so filled and overflowing, I could not contain myself.

"Thou wilt shew me the path of life:
in thy presence is fullness of joy;
at thy right hand there are pleasures for evermore." [22]

I had to smile and be happy. People who didn't know me, but had just seen me, approached me and said, "You seem to be so happy. Why is that?"

"But sanctify the Lord God in your hearts:
and be ready always to give an answer to every man
that asketh you a reason of the hope that is in you..." [23]

I have sometimes prayed that God would put a permanent smile and constant reflection of His love in my countenance, but realistically I am a serious-minded person and feel that God will always use that part of my character for His purposes.

This brings to mind another exhilarating facet of being a Christian. During Christian growth, just as in the A.A. Program, a person finds himself to be what the world would call a "hypocrite." The Bible tells me not to live as a hypocrite. It tells me that I won't be perfect until my last day. It also tells me, as Paul related to his previous state:

"For the good that I would I do not:
but the evil which I would not, that I do." [24]

And this is the Christian Liberation:

"O wretched man that I am! Who shall deliver me
from the body of this death? I thank God through Jesus Christ
our Lord. So then with the mind I serve the law of God;
but with the flesh the law of sin." [25]

God governs all my comings and goings. He establishes me and keeps me. He works in my life according to His will. He commands that I strive for perfection, that I run the race. He promises He will do the rest.

I make mistakes. I admit it. It is part of my promise to be honest as I write this book. It is my desire to tell it "the way it is."

I am concerned about witnessing to others, and I desire that God change me faster, so that I will be a more effective Christian.

This is the whole idea—that God wants to show how he can work in the life of a derelict and transform him. Praise God! The man I "was" is no longer and my ever-changing condition adds to my joy. I can't (and don't want to) rely on myself.

One of the benefits of my writing this book is the burning of bridges behind me. While I was in A.A., I had to do this to grow. It made things a lot easier once I cooperated with God's grace and exercised courage. I began to tell close associates, friends, and employers about my alcoholism. Yes, I knew that if I slipped, they would know where I was and what I was doing. But the Lord gave the grace to stay sober. This is a way of overcoming the bonds of fear, which try to keep one from stepping out and growing in enthusiasm and confidence. The Lord never fails me, and He will never fail you if you trust Him.

There will be future failures in my life, and when they occur, I will feel the strength of my conviction more than I do now. The Lord extends grace to help me overcome difficulties and grow to boundless victories in Him.

I am here to serve Him, which I find day by day is increasingly rewarding, although sometimes perplexing as well.

We are made wards of Jesus in the eyes of God. God knows all, but sees Jesus, time and again dust us off (His little ones) and present us to Him, in Jesus' name. In this way only is a sinner worthy to stand before God in petition. Prerequisites for appropriation from God, including repentance and forgiveness of sins, come only through Jesus Christ and the Word.

"...And let him that is athirst come. And whosoever will, let him take the water of life freely." [26]

We cannot imagine the great love God has for us because of our mortal limitations, through which we judge Him and others. The Bible tells of His love, and as we progress in the Word, we understand that love appreciatively and move beyond some of our limitations to be more like "Our Father."

"Because it is written, be ye holy; for I am holy." [27]

Chapter Two

Awareness

"Ask, and it shall be given you;
Seek, and ye shall find:
Knock, and it shall be opened unto you." [28]

RELIGIOUS VS. SPIRITUAL

One morning while going about my job, the Lord blessed my soul with joy in His fellowship. I felt His guidance and love and occasionally prayed quietly in the Spirit, in tongues.

I had once again been musing on the subject of religious versus spiritual experiences. In A.A. we realized that many of us had tried religion, but got drunk anyway. I realized that morning that I was associated with "religion" more than ever, but in a different way.

Yes, in the past I had tried religion but it didn't do much for me. Making the decision to give my life and my will to Jesus Christ, asking Him to come into my heart, and getting into the Word made all the difference. Once I sincerely repented, after having cried out in desperation, I had the real experience—by the grace of God. The decision went beyond submitting myself to God's will only until I received a favor or answer to a prayer.

The experience comes to each person differently, and this is the reason why it is called a personal experience with Christ, through the drawing of the Holy Spirit. I spent years of my life knowing *about* Jesus and I was taught the true *concept* of God. But without a commitment and first-hand knowledge of God's Word, the knowledge was comparatively fruitless. This is the reason why some persons reading this book will not be impressed by its contents unless they have the drawing of the Holy Spirit to their personal experience.

All things begin to fall into line and lead to an abundant life through the seeking of God via the Bible. However, this process is far from an automatic one. The Christian must learn the prerequisites for living a successful life in Christ, part of which is continued submission of one's will and the Christ-given power to rebuke evil intervention.

> *"Howbeit when he, the Spirit of truth, is come,*
> *he will guide you into all truth...."* [29]

One of the stumbling blocks encountered by new Christians is, "How will the Holy Spirit speak to me, or how will God show me these things?" There are many ways but primarily the Holy Spirit operates within a Christian through renewal of the mind—through study of the Bible.

> *"And be renewed in the spirit of your mind..."* [30]

Let's take a look at the words *religious* and *spiritual*.

Religious: *Man's beliefs with respect to powers and principalities of the universe*

Spiritual: *The motivating forces of a supernatural being, dealing with the mind*

The spiritual forces are the good forces from God and the evil forces from Satan.

Religion is no more than man's philosophy for living. Even liberalism is a religion. Religion alone can not accomplish much for the alcoholic or anyone in the spiritual realm. In seeking God, we subject our intellect, personality and will (our mind) to the good supernatural being for guidance.

This is a critical point because we are crying out to God to take over our will and our lives. This time occurs when spiritual forces war to take our minds. The more we work at it and the more we put into it, the greater the evil resistance, battle and rewards. The spiritual battle is waged between the Holy Spirit of God and evil spirits.

The reason the A.A. Program is so successful, I believe, is because it is God inspired and protected. Its precepts are based on the Word. The degree to which we exercise the precepts of A.A. determines, to an extent, how much progress we will make toward sobriety. Likewise, the extent to which a Christian embraces the Bible will determine how much progress he will make in spiritual growth and what degree of experience he will encounter or gain.

One of the most important things in this book, if not *the* most important, are these words: **"The success of your sobriety or of your Christian life depends on how much of the Bible, God's word, becomes a part of your spiritual being."**

As we enter the critical point at the time of turning our wills and our lives over to the care of God, we find many influences that tend to draw us in one direction or another, if we are truly seeking God's will for our lives. My experience at this point was a couple of years of frustration.

Following the Program kept me sober, but there were too many periods of feeling low, experiencing a lack of joy, and also a realization that I was still seeking.

Things had not come together yet and were not to do so for some time. God had truly done remarkable works in my life, but during this time I did not consciously experience the

Word of God. It was not until the time that I got my first Bible, began to read it, study it, and expose myself to the workings of the Holy Spirit of God that I made genuine progress and saw the reality of God in my life.

The important fact is that many people don't know that the A.A. Program is based on the Bible. I had been subjected to the intent of the Word of God in the Program, but did not make the discovery until a few years later. I came to realize that God had been working in my life, by His Word, without my even knowing it!

> *"I cried by reason of mine affliction unto the Lord,*
> *and he heard me; out of the belly of hell cried I,*
> *and thou heardest my voice!"* [31]

He protected me, cared for me, taught me and brought me to the place, by His Holy Spirit, where I consciously endeavored to live in His Word.

It is true that I am relating to "religion" more than ever. The reason is that now my religion is based upon the manifested Word of God. And that Word *is* God!

In God's time, He led me into His truth and I became part of His true Church. My story is uniquely mine, as your story is in accordance with God's plan for your life.

Anyone who seeks Him and is willing to repent can go on to find the meaning of God's Church, a part of the bride of Christ.

God did not intend for there to be church*es*. As it turned out, man created many "churches" of various religions. These religions have partly been established and differ because of man's desire for his own beliefs by which to live. Some churches are a variation or deviation from the original intent of the Church of our Lord.

Going to church once a week to pay homage to God was based on religion—keeping the Sabbath as prescribed by man's laws. Not having a Bible, I was living a theoretical spirituality. Today, with the Bible as my personal contact with God, I know that the Sabbath was made for man—not man for the Sabbath. I know the Christian is free to hold any day as the Sabbath, doing good works on any day, as Christ did. All Sabbaths were only symbolic of the constant rest now available in Jesus.

John the Baptist, who paved the way for Jesus, taught repentance.

"Repent ye, for the kingdom of heaven is at hand." [32]

He proceeded to baptize, encouraging the confession of sins.

When Jesus began His public ministry, He started with the same quote. Jesus then called together a group of men called the apostles.

"Follow me and I will make you fishers of men." [33]

God intended for a Church to be established. This was done by Jesus.

"And I say also unto thee, that thou art Peter,
and upon this rock (Jesus) I will build my church." [34]

After the death and Resurrection of Christ, He commissioned the Church to go and teach all nations;

"...baptizing them in the name of the Father,
and of the Son, and of the Holy Ghost.
Teaching them to observe all things
whatsoever I have commanded you.
And lo, I will be with you alway,
even unto the end of the world." [35]

In the period between 1960 and 1970, a spiritual revival was again arising and the Lord was pouring out an extra measure of His Holy Spirit. The outpouring was evidenced by the speaking in tongues, such as that which occurred at Pentecost, and was the bonding agent that was falling on all denominational churches, because people were "thirsting."

"...if any man thirst, let him come unto me, and drink.
He that believeth on me, as the scripture hath said,
out of his belly shall flow rivers of living water.
But this he spake of the Spirit,
which they that believe on him should receive:
for the Holy Ghost was not yet given;
because that Jesus was not yet glorified." [36]

The outpouring was controlled by God and was manifested in all denominations, yet religious man continued to deny its reality. Many preachers still preach today that the outpouring was only for the early Church.

Denominations that did not believe in tongues were disturbed because of the outpouring. "Pentecostals" were reevaluating their position because God was revealing the fact that the Baptism of the Holy Spirit accompanied by the evidence of tongues was just the beginning of the total commitment, and that many were walking in a degree of unbelief and spiritual poverty.

Pentecost is not a denomination. It consists of the Baptism of the Holy Spirit with the evidence of speaking in tongues and the practice of all the gifts to the Church, including divine healing.

The falling of Pentecost is one reason why it is so exciting to be a Christian at anytime. It is stimulating to see our Lord work in all denominations through manifestation of the Pentecostal experience. There is an anticipation of bringing the Church together, eliminating the man-made elements.

Pentecostal churches are not religion-free either, but God's manifestations confirm the full gospel, Spirit-led approach.

I pray that the operation of the gifts to the Church be returned in full power through the obedience of our Lord's command for repentance and reverent worship.

I am not promoting denominational membership, but rather, Jesus for everyone, in the heart. I pray that God will unite all Christians around that theme.

There are lessons to be learned in love and closer communication in interdenominational realms. I pray that growth will continue in these areas for the glory of God.

FORTY YEARS IN THE DESERT

I lived almost forty years before I found God Real!—despite the fact that I had been acquainted with Him since childhood. What made the difference? These things occurred:

1. I cried out to God sincerely.

2. I took all the Steps in A.A. with true repentance.

3. I earnestly prayed for His true concept.

4. I heard the plan of salvation.

5. I consciously accepted Jesus and eternal life.

6. I began to read the Bible.

7. I began to believe in the Word.

8. I had a real experience with Christ.

Many times I had cried out to God. Many times I had begged Him to help me. The simple fact was that I hadn't known how to approach the Throne. How did I come to know? I came to know through true initial repentance and (subconsciously) through other of God's commands in the Program of A.A.

In the Program, I was taught how to learn, how to live, how to seek a simple way of life, how to simplify all things in my life. In the Program, God was simply "God." But beyond that point, something—and I know that was the Holy Spirit—prompted me to realize that God was more.

I spent hours in a little Peach Street apartment in Arlington, Texas, praying for God's true concept, a closer walk, His reality, and the actual meaning of life.

Evil forces being active, as well as the Holy Spirit, spiritual oversimplification might have become detrimental.

I had been taught the Trinity of God—the Father, Son, and the Holy Spirit. But in my efforts to simplify everything in my life, including God, that I might live a reasonable, peaceful, sane life, I began to wonder about the Trinity.

I believe this is the place where God put His hand on the situation and stopped the process. He was not going to permit me to go any further in simplification. Having trusted God to the best of my ability, I felt that His placing His hand on my life at that particular time was further confirmation that He was directing my steps.

Many of these things I did not know at the time, but as I look back, I can see how God brought me along. This is the kind of thing that lets me know that God set up the Program to bring derelicts up from the bottom and into the fullness of Christ.

Shortly thereafter, in Plymouth Park Baptist Church in Irving, Texas, I listened to and received God's revelation of the plan of salvation for mankind.

About that time, a whole new meaning began to come into my life. Actually the process had started a while back, but was advancing. There was the increasing tempo of spiritual battles and a prelude to spiritual adventures in the future.

Although my salvation came a little at a time, rather than at the altar, or in some other way, it came through developing a conscious contact with God as prescribed in the Steps of A.A., and walking close to the Lord. It came through consciously accepting Him and developing a fellowship with Him. This led to a conviction of salvation within my spirit, for which I have always been grateful.

I publicly accepted Christ in response to a salvation invitation during a service at Plymouth Park Baptist, and thereafter began to read the Bible regularly. A craving for the Word began to set in, sometimes more intense than others, but for the first time the Word of God—the Bible—began to have meaning to me. A little here and a little there; but nevertheless, it was a big thing for me to begin to understand it.

My adventure began by small scale experimentation with God's Word and snowballed into miracles, by believing.

I look back and wonder why it took so long. I can only guess that the Lord had things to work out in my life, to prepare me for my new adventure. Perhaps God wanted me in a position where I would be willing to hearken to His immediate commands, so that I might advance. **I had to learn that suffering or affliction is no ticket to free license.**

The two-year period after taking the Steps was a period of difficulty and growth. Enough difficulty that growth resulted, and this was at least encouraging, yet not so much so that I was ready to give up at any time. If I had relied more on God, I could have better endured the hardships.

Hardships changed to adventures! Praise God for the work He has done and is doing in my life. I would not trade anything for the progress that has taken place since I sat at the kitchen table looking at the Twelve Steps for the first time and "knew that I was hopelessly lost and beyond recovery."

The Lord put me through the Program and brought me to the place where I could begin my walk with Him. Is your present "place" perhaps God's call to a walk with Him—in Christ?

God Talks to Us

"That they should seek the Lord,
if haply they might feel after him, and find him,
though he be not far from every one of us." [37]

I believe that God speaks to man by the following nine methods because they are all Scriptural and factual. The Lord has spoken to me in some of these ways; therefore, He has proven to me that He does communicate with man:

1. Through the Word

2. By impression on the mind, including mental visions

3. Tongues and interpretations

4. Prophecy

5. Spiritual visions

6. Angelic visits

7. Dreams

8. Audibly

9. Circumstances and facts of answered prayers

Through the Word

The Bible is the most important means of communication between God and His People. Therefore Christians should daily read and study the Word, as God's voice, and make it a part of their being.

Because the Bible states God's will for our lives, we need only extract from it and apply it. A person will seek answers in vain if the answers are already in the Word and the person chooses to reject them or not apply them.

I speak from experience when I say that the Lord will let you know how much effort is required on your part to get the answers by this method. The Lord will direct any new Christian to those specific Scriptures wherein answers will be found, just as He did for me. This is an exciting time in a Christian's growth. As Christians mature and become more familiar with the Word, they then will have the knowledge of what particular part of the Bible holds the answers they seek.

This communication consists of more than just reading the Bible. It includes meditation and the Holy Spirit's enlightenment of the mind, to make It's meaning known to the Christian. These same revelations cannot be known or understood by a person without a personal commitment to Christ.

"Now we have received, not the spirit of the world,
but the spirit which is of God;
that we might know the things
that are freely given to us of God." [38]

Impression on the Mind

One method of communication is when the Lord impresses my mind with things He wants me to know. Impressions on the mind are many and the Word of God sifts out the error. Impressions often come as Scriptural quotes and sometimes as mental visions. Many of my impressions have been followed by confirmation.

Tongues and Interpretation

Tongues is usually a language known only to God. On occasion, the Holy Spirit will speak in a known language through a person who does not know the language. Tongues is the evidence of receiving the baptism of the Holy Spirit, also known as the Pentecostal experience. All Christians receive the Spirit of God and a measure of anointing, but the baptism of the Holy Spirit is an additional infilling or anointing for doing the works of Christ and the apostles.

Some of the results of that anointing in my life are the writing of this book and the privilege of witnessing and praying with dozens of people, one on one, to accept Jesus Christ. Other results are illustrated throughout this book.

A person who receives the baptism of the Holy Spirit with the evidence of tongues goes on to pray in tongues in subsequent personal prayer. Tongues range from a clear, precise sounding language to a ridiculous sounding babbling. Sometimes it is mixed with weeping, gasping, or whatever the effects of the power of the Holy Spirit are upon the person.

Tongues are divided into two categories:

1. Tongues is the language spoken as evidence of the Holy Spirit Baptism, which result in a personal ministry of intercession, devotion, rest, strength and faith.

2. Tongues is the language spoken in tongues and interpretations. It is the speaking in tongues that may come forth during a church service or other Christian gathering. This is termed a message in tongues and, when interpreted, results in edification of the church body, and in ministering to God and the congregation, including the items of ministry in the above

personal ministry. Only this category is the "gift" of tongues.

When a member of the congregation is given the *meaning* of a message in tongues and speaks it forth in the assembly, under the power of the Holy Spirit, this is known as the interpretation. The two combined is tongues and interpretation. Thus God speaks to His Church first by using the physical body: the tongue, lips, vocal chords, all speaking faculties of a person; then, by giving the message in the local language through the same person or another person.

Tongues and interpretation often determine the trend of a Pentecostal church service. For example: A church service may be changed from a worshipping service to one of a call for salvation. Some church services are primarily worshipful in nature. These services minister to the Lord by praising and loving Him. The Lord ministers to the congregation with blessings of the fruit of the Spirit, freedom from the bondage of fear and other evils. People receive healings. At dismissal of the service, the entire church body has been edified and has received blessings from the Lord. At other times the worship service may be interrupted, in an orderly way, with a message of tongues and interpretation. Therein the minister will change the service to one of a plea for a person who may need Christ, or who may be in some conflict or spiritual need, as indicated by the message.

In the past, many denominations have rejected members who began speaking in tongues. Since the outpourings, however, some are starting to recognize the reality of tongues.

> *"With men of other tongues and other lips*
> *will I speak unto this people;*
> *and yet for all that will they not hear me, saith the Lord.*

Wherefore tongues are for a sign, not to them that believe,
but to them that believe not:
prophesying serveth not for them that believe not,
but for them which believe." [39]

Tongues sounds peculiar because it is peculiar. The message sometimes comes forth in a known foreign language. It will be understood by some individual in the service who knows the foreign language, even though it is unknown to the speaker.

Prophecy

Prophecy is a message from God, by the Holy Spirit, through a person, in the local language. Prophecy comes forth in the same manner as interpretation, except that it is a proclamation rather than an interpretation.

Spiritual Visions

Spiritual visions are the placing of a picture before man's eyes by God.

During my personal vision experience, I prayed for God to be real to me, but I was still very surprised and shaken at His response because I did not know that He would show me a vision. Neither had God ever spoken to me or been that real to me before.

Seeing a vision does not mean that a person is exceptionally holy or spiritually outstanding. Some people have testified to having visions, which were admonitions to them, because they needed to repent of their evil ways. I have heard testimonies of spiritual visions of a prolonged nature, wherein the Lord has shown Christians many things, some of which went beyond this life. My limited experience with visions prohibits me from expounding further.

Angelic Visits

This is a communication in which an angel appears on Earth to help manifest the Lord's purpose, such as the appearance of an angel at the sepulcher where Jesus had been laid.

> *"And, behold, there was a great earthquake:*
> *for the angel of the Lord descended from heaven,*
> *and came and rolled back the stone from the door,*
> *and sat upon it."* [40]

Dreams

Dreams are the most difficult form of God's communication for man to properly interpret. This is an area where "self" gets into the act and the enemy will try hard to intervene. A person should be careful to make particular tests and wait for God's confirmation to determine whether the events of the dream are from God, the enemy, or the self.

There are numerous examples of dreams in the Scriptures. Several of these are found in the first chapters of Matthew. God spoke to Joseph, via an angel, through a dream, informing him that Mary had conceived of the Holy Spirit.

Audibly

In the ninth chapter of Acts, Saul, a murderer of Christians, was on his way to Damascus to find Christians whom he might arrest and take back to Jerusalem. Saul fell to the ground, under the power of God. He heard the Lord speak to him saying,

"Saul, Saul, why do you persecute me?" [41]

This was the time God had chosen for Saul to do His work. During this incident, Saul was temporarily stricken blind by God. In Damascus, a man named Ananias was given a spiritual vision by God, in which he was instructed to pray for Saul, that his eyes might be restored. Ananias prayed and on the third day after Saul's arrival in Damascus Saul's eyesight was restored. In these incidents, God contacted man audibly and through a spiritual vision.

"And it shall come to pass in the last days, saith God,
I will pour out my spirit upon all flesh:
and your sons and your daughters shall prophecy,
and your young men shall see visions,
and your old men shall dream dreams...." [42]

Circumstances and Facts of Answered Prayer

The Lord lets us know His will by answering prayers, even though, sometimes it is not in accordance with our desires. This method of communication is often very direct and decisive. These are times when we have to evaluate, not on the basis of feelings, but on the basis of facts.

This is another area where accuracy sometimes becomes difficult because of the enemy's ability to create confusion in our minds. The Christian has to test out this method, just as in the case of dreams.

One can eliminate a lot of frustration and error in seeking answers from God by simply believing God will answer and then letting God select the method. Action is not recommended, on any method, until God has repeatedly confirmed that method and comfortably established it as a means of communication with the individual.

TWELVE STEPS TOWARD LIBERTY

The following are the Twelve Steps of the A.A. Program, as listed in the "Big Book".*

1. We admitted we were powerless over alcohol—that our lives had become unmanageable.

2. Came to believe that a Power greater than ourselves could restore us to sanity.

3. Made a decision to turn our will and our lives over to the care of God <u>as we understood Him</u>.

4. Made a searching and fearless moral inventory of ourselves.

5. Admitted to God, to ourselves, and to another human being the exact nature of our wrongs.

6. Were entirely ready to have God remove all these defects of character.

7. Humbly asked Him to remove our shortcomings.

8. Made a list of all persons we had harmed, and become willing to make amends to them all.

9. Made direct amends to such people wherever possible, except when to do so would injure them or others.

---

* "The Big Book" refers to the book *Alcoholics Anonymous* (New York: Alcoholics Anonymous World Services, Inc., 1976).

The Twelve Steps are reprinted with permission of Alcoholics Anonymous World Services, Inc. Permission to reprint the Twelve Steps does not mean that A.A. has reviewed or approved the contents of this publication, nor that A.A. agrees with the views expressed herein. A.A. is a program of recovery from alcoholism <u>only</u> – use of the Twelve Steps in connection with programs and activities which are patterned after A.A., but which address other problems or concerns, or in any other non-A.A. context, does not imply otherwise.

10. Continued to take personal inventory and when we were wrong promptly admitted it.

11. Sought through prayer and meditation to improve our conscious contact with God <u>as we understood Him</u>, praying only for knowledge of His will for us and the power to carry that out.

12. Having had a spiritual awakening as the result of these steps, we tried to carry this message to alcoholics and to practice these principles in all our affairs.

Scriptural quotations and comments given below, concerning the Twelve Steps, are the author's and are not to be misconstrued as those of A.A. These Scriptures and comments are given to show similarity between The Twelve Steps and The Word of God.

1) *"O our God, wilt thou not judge them? for we have no might against this great company that cometh against us; neither know we what to do: but our eyes are upon thee."* [43]

"Not that we are sufficient of ourselves to think anything as of ourselves; but our sufficiency is of God." [44]

2) *"...If thou canst believe, all things are possible to him that believeth."* [45]

"I can do all things through Christ which strengtheneth me." [46]

"...go thy way, thy faith hath made thee whole." [47]

3) *"And if it seem evil unto you to serve the Lord, choose you this day whom ye will serve; whether the Gods which your fathers served that were on the other side of the floods, or the Gods of the Amorites, in whose land ye dwell; but as for me and my house, we will serve the Lord."* [48]

"...How long halt ye between two opinions? If the Lord be of God, follow him; but if Baal, then follow him." [49]

4) *"Let us search and try our ways, and turn again to the Lord."* [50]

"Cast away from you all your transgressions, whereby ye have transgressed; and make you a new heart and a new spirit...." [51]

5) *"Now therefore make confession unto the Lord God of your fathers, and do his pleasure..."* [52]

"Confess your faults one to another, and pray one for another, that ye may be healed." [53]

6) *"Thy Kingdom come, Thy will be done in earth, as it is in heaven."* [54]

7) *"Lord thou has heard the desire of the humble: thou wilt prepare their heart, thou wilt cause thine ear to hear."* [55]

"Humble yourselves therefore under the mighty hand of God, that he may exalt you in due time...." [56]

8) *"Forbearing one another, and forgiving one another, if any man have a quarrel against any; even as Christ forgave you, so also do ye."* [57]

9) *"And forgive us our debts, as we forgive our debtors."* [58]

"Therefore if thou bring thy gift to the altar, and there rememberest that thy brother hath ought against thee; leave there thy gift before the altar, and go thy way; first be reconciled to thy brother, and then come and offer thy gift." [59]

10) *"He that covereth his sins shall not prosper: but whoso confesseth and forsaketh them shall have mercy."* [60]

11) *"Seek the Lord, and his strength: seek his face evermore."* [61]

12) *"...Go ye into all the world, and preach the gospel to every creature."* [62]

"Thou therefore which teachest another, teachest thou not thyself: Thou that preachest a man should not steal, does thou steal?" [63]

After reviewing the Twelve Steps in a scriptural light, we can see the similarity.

The point I wish to make is this: We have really only taken the first step. There is much more in the way of improving one's spirituality and so much more to gain in the rewards of believing in Jesus Christ and the gospel, instead of simply

"God." Many of the rewards you will see in the experiences I will share in this book.

EMOTIONAL STRESS AND SPIRITUAL BATTLES

In order to realize significant growth, a person must go through emotional changes. People are basically opposed to any kind of a change in their lives. Most find that life is hard to live, hard to face. When confronted with God's miracles, it is an impossible feat to absorb them without experiencing great emotion. They are difficult to comprehend when most of our lives we have been used to a theoretical existence of Him.

During the transition from living a worldly existence prior to one's acceptance of Christ to becoming a Christian and having a genuine experience, we go through periods when we are confronted with what we feel are severe emotional seasons. At those times we may decide against further progress in getting to the place where we ought to be, in Christ.

Some of my battles came when the Lord gave me a vision of Sodom and Gomorrah. This was because of minor superstitions and beliefs instilled during my past life, which were of man, not of God; and because of fear due to evil influences.

A good fear will keep a person from walking into the path of an automobile. This is the God-given kind. The evil kind is meant to discourage the authenticity of God. In being confronted with the reality of God, many fears loom forth.

"Perhaps I will suffer material loss."

"What will my friends or relatives think?"

"What if God should let me down?"

"I might make a fool of myself."

"Maybe I am getting into something evil."

"Maybe God will punish me for leaving my religion."

"I will have to give up things."

I lived with all these fears, but the Lord protected me and gave me the grace to overcome them.

"For God hath not given us the spirit of fear; but of power, and of love, and of a sound mind." [64]

"My grace is sufficient for thee: for my strength is made perfect in weakness." [65]

We all want love, joy, peace, and all the other fruit of the Spirit, but we have to get the Spirit of Christ first! The only way to that which we all desire is through Jesus Christ and the gospel!

I fought many battles and experienced a great deal of emotional upheaval until I decided to simply rely on God and trust Him in all things, to the best of my ability.

Through spiritual encounters I walked as God's child. Seeking Him through the Word, I found that He always led me, as I kept my mind on Him and sought His way.

Eventually, I prayed, "Lord, I know that you keep me; I trust You completely." I proceeded to let God do what He would; while, at the same time, I verified things by the Word and their "harmony with the gospel."

What I mean by "the harmony of the gospel," in this instance, is the fact that all things that God does, and all things that make up a real Christian experience, are harmonious. They are not conflicting or confusing; they are satisfying.

The Lord verified my stand with such Scriptures as:

"Or if he ask a fish, will he give him a serpent?" [66]

"But the Lord is faithful, who shall establish you, and keep you from evil." [67]

Satan met total defeat in the Crucifixion and Resurrection of Jesus Christ, not knowing it would be his doom. Satan never had the power to take the life of Christ. Christ voluntarily gave His life so that the enemy might be defeated, the Scripture might be fulfilled and we might have salvation. After His resurrection, Jesus appeared unto the disciples saying,

"All power is given unto me in heaven and in earth." [68]

The Christian has the same power available and may do even greater things.

"He that believeth on me, the works that I do shall he do also; and greater works than these shall he do;..." [69]

What the Lord has done in my life to date convinces me of the infallibility of the Word.

When the Lord directs a Christian in a miraculous work, He gives witness to the person's spirit so that the person has the boldness to perform the act, in the name of Jesus Christ.

Part of the power that is given to the Christian is the power to rebuke the enemy, Satan. The power of Christ is within the Christian. I have had sufficient experience to know it and believe it.

"Lord, even the devils are subject unto us through thy name." [70]

"Behold, I give unto you power to tread on serpents and scorpions, and over all the power of the enemy: and nothing shall by any means hurt you." [71]

I've had victories because I dared to fight the spiritual battles required, and won. This is spiritual warfare.

The work that God does in us is a process of controlled "self" destruction, which is accomplished as we yield to the Holy Spirit, recognize our shortcomings and permit Him to work in our lives, toward perfection. We are overcoming the "old man," permitting God to destroy him, in the "flesh."

We are being made new and begin to recognize past hang-ups and impulse actions we have practiced since our childhood.

Many of us have tried self-improvement techniques, which may have helped to some extent. But genuine progress comes on "The potter's wheel"—the things God does to make us rely on Him. These are miracles that make us eager to go against "self" nature. They are the things that show advancement and spiritual value.

Along the way, we sometimes have doubts because of our temporary misunderstanding of the gospel. But the Lord always helps us through these spots by revealing more to us and strengthening us.

Now we rejoice in times of tribulation, wherein we used to be exceedingly distraught. We pray for others' salvation and rejoice at their "going home to be with the Lord" when they leave us behind, because we know of their eternal life, which will be the same as ours.

The Christian's weapon is the Word of God.

"And take the helmet of salvation, and the sword of the Spirit, which is the word of God." [72]

Satan and all his evil spirits hate the precious blood of Jesus, and when it is used by the Christian, this is what drives them away, subdues them, and stops their oppression. Binding Satan and his evil spirits by the blood of Jesus, they can be made to cease working on a person or his life.

*"...and whatsoever thou shalt bind on earth
shall be bound in heaven:
and whatsoever thou shalt loose on earth
shall be loosed in heaven."* [73]

Followed by this, a Christian prays to God and asks Him to touch that person or situation in the name of Jesus Christ.

By the same token, threatened illnesses are controlled. On numerous occasions since I accepted Christ, I have been threatened with illnesses that usually have kept me bedridden for days. Now I rebuke them and ask the Lord to heal me and keep me healthy. I give Him all the glory for the good health He has given me.

> *"Who his own self bare our sins in his own body on the tree,*
> *that we, being dead to sins, should live unto righteousness;*
> *by whose stripes ye were healed." [74]*

Sometimes we may feel we are expected to suffer some afflictions, so that God may have His way. But my attitude is to fight any illness and to thank God for His mercy and goodness, as He continues to bless me.

The Lord is ever-present with the Christian. The Christian has available power over the enemy and must learn to use it in daily battle. Some do not understand why they have such oppressions with Christ ever present. What needs to be understood is that the enemy is defeated on every occasion when the Christian exercises the authority and power, but the Lord does not initiate the action. After rebuking and binding the enemy, by the blood of Jesus Christ, then the Lord finishes the work. It works every time though the battle be short-term or prolonged. When the Christian allows the oppression to grow to the point of discouragement (unbelief), the battle is lost and victory is not attained. This is one area where praying in tongues is invaluable to the Christian.

Constantly, the Holy Spirit works to transform the Christian's mind. At the same time, the enemy tries to oppress the mind and hinder the Christian's progress. Through the Scriptures, I have had many battles, made progress and have had my faith strengthened. I have used the above Scriptures many times and felt the peace of God flood over my soul and remove fears, tensions, and anxieties. From this standpoint, Christians cannot afford to be slack in learning the Word as God brings them along.

People are suffering unnecessary oppression, trying to get through life on tranquilizers and other mind-altering medications. Many are being freed by the blood of Christ.

It is so important that a Christian confess positive things through speech. It is obvious that people are not living victorious Christian lives by the evidence of their daily confession. By this I mean the dark, oppressed, negative outlook observed in conversation.

> *"Thou are snared with the words of thy mouth,*
> *thou art taken with the words of thy mouth."* [75]

For the healing of bursitis, which was my first major healing, I professed healing for three months and never once wavered in my words that Jesus had healed me.

Fear is the dominant weapon of the enemy. The name and blood of Jesus are the dominant weapons of the Christian.

> *"Ye are of God, little children, and have overcome them:*
> *because greater is he that is in you,*
> *than he that is in the world."* [76]

GOD'S ETERNAL PLAN FOR YOU

God's eternal plan was completely unknown to me prior to my spiritual experience. I learned of it through the Bible and diligent seeking of God.

You have often heard about the final days of the world. Many scoff saying, "Yeah, people have said that for years."

"But, beloved, be not ignorant of this one thing, that one day is with the Lord as a thousand years, and a thousand years as one day." [77]

It is true, no one knows when the last day will come, but it is not wise to play roulette, waiting for it. The "last days" have been nearly two thousand years, since the birth of Christ. It may be just a few hours, it may be years. Christ has come and fulfilled the Scriptures. Scriptures say that the end of this era is near.

Every person is included in the Eternal Plan of God, just as each has a time of crisis, a time of decision, a time of eternal loss or gain. Every one of us stands in the same place in God's eyes: in His plan!

Some of us become alcoholics. This happens to pull us out persuasively, that we might be set apart by God. We are chosen out of utter helplessness by Him and given a testimony that enables us to know His reality and love and to share it with others.

There are many steps in God's Eternal Plan, and we are close to the final chapter of the current age. I speak with reference to the Holy Bible's book of Revelation.

God's Eternal Plan

God Created Heaven and Earth

Satan Dethroned for Trying to Rise Above God

Adam and Eve Put on Earth, Their Downfall

World Destroyed Except for Noah and the Ark

Moses and the Ten Commandments

The Coming of Christ – The Dispensation of Grace

Descent of the Holy Ghost

Rapture of the Church

Seven Years of Tribulation

The Second Coming of Christ

Millennium

God-Magog, Satan's Last Revolt

Renovation of the Earth

The Perfect Age

I will not comment on the events that took place prior to The Coming of Christ and the current Dispensation of Grace or "Church Age." They are recorded in the Bible for those who seek to know them. The thing to be aware of now is the coming Rapture of the Church.

The Coming of Christ, The Dispensation of Grace

This was and is the age in which Jesus came and walked the Earth as a man, the Son of God, and who came to reconcile all with God, by His grace, through the power of His Resurrection. This is also called the "Church Age."

All these years, God has been working in men's lives to eliminate rebellion against Him, to save those who "will let" Him and to bring all things under subjection to Himself.

> *"Forasmuch as ye know that ye were not redeemed*
> *with corruptible things, as silver and gold,*
> *from your vain conversation received by tradition*
> *from your fathers; but with the precious blood of Christ,*
> *as of a lamb without blemish and without spot:*
> *Who verily was ordained before the foundation of the world,*
> *but was manifest in these last days for you,*
> *Who by him do believe in God,*
> *that raised him up from the dead,*
> *and gave him glory;*
> *that your faith and hope might be in God." [78]*

By these Scriptures, we see that God manifested Jesus Christ as our Saviour. In recorded history, Jesus is the only person of a "Godhead" who died, was resurrected and was seen by many afterwards. If any other "God" was presented as "alive," there is no proof of it.

Descent of the Holy Ghost

Jesus commanded the apostles to wait for the promise of the Father—the coming of the Holy Ghost and power, which would come after the Ascension of Jesus into Heaven.

"It is not for you to know the times or the season,
which the Father hath put in his own power.
But ye shall receive power, after that the Holy Ghost
is come upon you: and ye shall be witnesses unto me
both in Jerusalem, and in all Judea, and in all Samaria,
and unto the uttermost part of the earth.
And when he had spoken these things, while they beheld,
he was taken up; and a cloud received him out of their sight." [79]

The following Scriptures give the account of the Holy Ghost's descent after Christ ascended (or was taken up) into heaven and the outpouring of the Holy Spirit to this present day.

"And when the day of Pentecost was fully come,
they were with one accord in one place.
And suddenly there came a sound from heaven
as of a rushing mighty wind, and it filled all the house
where they were sitting. And there appeared unto them
cloven tongues as of fire, and it sat upon each of them.
And they were all filled with the Holy Ghost,
and began to speak with other tongues,
as the Spirit gave them utterance..." [80]

"And it shall come to pass in the last days, saith God,
I will pour out my Spirit upon all flesh:

and your sons and your daughters shall prophesy,
and your young men shall see visions, and your old men
shall dream dreams: And on my servants
and on my handmaidens I will pour out in those days
of my Spirit; and they shall prophesy.” [81]

“...And it shall come to pass, that whosoever shall call on
the name of the Lord shall be saved.” [82]

The Lord is still pouring out His Spirit upon the Church, as He said He would in the above Scriptures, to those who would seek until they obtain. Revival movements spring up in all religions, privileging all seekers to find God's fullness and become “one” by worshipping Jesus in their hearts, in a like manner. The Kingdom of Heaven is the place to which they are being pointed and the heart is the place where the Kingdom of God resides. Religions will remain as man's way and the true Church will be “pulled” out as its members will let, to be made ready, as part of the bride of Christ.

“That he might present it to himself a glorious church,
not having spot, or wrinkle, or any such thing;
but that it should be holy and without blemish.” [83]

Likewise, spiritual perverts are being given up unto their own heart's lust. They will receive their just reward—the tribulation and the second death.

Many see these latter day events all around them yet reject them and refuse to investigate or acknowledge the confirming of the Scriptures. It's going to continue until the Rapture of the Church; it cannot be stopped.

Rapture of the Church

The very next occurrence will be the Rapture of the Church. The Rapture will be "it," as far as earthly trials are concerned for the Christian, the person who has accepted Christ and run the race.

At the time of the Rapture, Christians will physically rise to meet Christ in the air, preceded by the dead in Christ of all ages.

"For the Lord himself shall descend from Heaven with a shout, with the voice of the Archangel, and with the trump of God; and the dead in Christ shall rise first:
Then we which are alive and remain shall be caught up together with them in the clouds, to meet the Lord in the air: and so shall we ever be with the Lord." [84]

Seven Years of Tribulation

Those who have not accepted Christ will continue on Earth during the seven years of tribulation.

During a five-month period of this era, men will be horribly tormented by demons in various forms but will not be able to die—by suicide or any other means.

"And in those days shall men seek death, and shall not be able to find it; and shall desire to die, and death shall flee from them." [85]

There will be open sin and plagues, including famine and earthquakes.

"And I beheld when he had opened the sixth seal, and, lo,
there was a great earthquake; and the sun became black
as sackcloth of hair, and the moon became as blood;
and the stars of heaven fell unto the earth...." [86]

The entire solar system will be disturbed. One third of the sun, moon, and stars will be destroyed. The Earth will have numerous periods of total darkness during the daylight hours. Men and water life will perish from polluted water.

The anti-Christ will have a free hand to reign with sin. Some will accept the mark of the beast and be heirs of Satan. Others will reject it and become martyred Christians.

The tribulation will be the worst kind of "purgatory" one can go through.

The Second Coming of Christ

Christ will return to Jerusalem with Christians of all ages— those resurrected from the graves (first resurrection) and those raptured from the Earth.

Those who will have accepted the mark of the beast and are alive at the end of the tribulation will be slain and devoured by fire.

The Anti-Christ and the False Prophet will be cast into the lake of fire.

Millennium

The raptured Christians and those of the first resurrection (during the Rapture) will be like Christ and will reign with Him. They will be non-marrying and non-reproducing and will rule over those who will have rejected the mark of the beast and been martyred. The martyred people will be able to continue to reproduce through the Millennium and on into the New Earth since they will not have been resurrected or raptured.

During this thousand year Millennium, Satan will be bound. Those who had died in the tribulation, having accepted the mark of the beast, will remain dead through the millennium.

Unlike the present age, there will be no evil influence on Earth, and the lamb will lie down with the lion.

Gog-Magog, Satan's Last Revolt

Satan will be loosed and will deceive others, after Christ's one thousand year reign. Those deceived will join his army and will be consumed by fire.

The remaining dead unbelievers will be judged (second resurrection). Those not in the book of life will be cast into the lake of fire (second death).

Satan will also be cast into the lake of fire.

Renovation of the Earth

Heaven and Earth will be purified with fire and re-formed.

The Perfect Age

All things will be restored as they were before sin entered

the world, in Genesis. The Christians will reign under God. The "natural" people, those martyred Christians from the tribulation, will be the ruled inhabitants of the New Earth.

> *"And God shall wipe away all tears from their eyes;*
> *and there shall be no more death, neither sorrow, nor crying,*
> *neither shall there be any more pain:*
> *for the former things are passed away."* [87]

The glory of God (not the sun or moon) will light the Earth eternally!

Chapter Three

Adventure Begins

"I press toward the mark for the prize
of the high calling of God in Christ Jesus." [88]

JUST KEEP WALKING

After taking Step Three in the A.A. Program and continuing to work the other Steps, I began tuning in station G-O-D as never before.

I had always believed in Jesus Christ's becoming man and being resurrected. Now the time had come for me to be drawn closer to God, by the Holy Spirit and the Word.

I embarked on a new adventure. The same world, the same life, the same person were changing rapidly in the ensuing months and years. The boredom of my humdrum existence was ending and a new adventure was about to begin.

A complete upheaval of my life occurred in 1969, in which my job, family, friends, and most material relationships were severed.

I believe this separation happened partly because of my complete surrender to God in the prevailing situation. Fighting for sobriety, for my very life, I found things to be unbearable, within the limitations of my own strength, and I had little hope for the future. Surrenduring the situation to God, I prayed, "Lord, if this is what you want for my life, I will stick with it. I will endure anything. Just grant me the strength to endure, to go on."

As soon as I surrendered to the situation, I was removed from it. An unsolicited divorce and a job layoff were the major items that instigated the changes. But many new things began to open up, such as travel. I began to feel a greater release from fears, from that which had held me down for years.

The ensuing period included extensive time alone with God. I look upon that particular time as a great blessing, for it severed me from the world that I had to be separated from in order to grow in Christ.

The Lord did it in such a way that it was a beautiful experience. I was given a traveling retreat—driving across the States to my new job. During this time I prayed, drew closer to God, and spent many bittersweet hours. They were bitter because of the severance I was experiencing from the materialistic, worldly existence that I had clung to. They were sweet, because the Lord's hand was on me. I felt His closeness. He held me up and gave me joy and peace.

There were times after driving for hours that I would drive off the road into the desert, or wherever I might be. I would get out of the car and sit or walk and talk to God. This in itself was a whole new experience for me.

I knew that under the circumstances I was doing the best that I could to walk in His will. I continuously felt a release from anxieties, tensions and fears that had gripped my existence for years. In the past I had passed through many trials unaware of what was happening. Many times on Redondo Beach, California, I repeated the same question, "Lord, what's it all about?" Sitting in the presence of God, with tear-filled eyes, unhappiness of a kind inside, it was just as if a peace-producing voice was leading me so tenderly, saying, "It's all right, John, just keep walking."

One Saturday afternoon in El Segundo, California, while still in the Catholic Church, I went to confession. I was in need of someone to discuss my difficulties with; I needed a good listener.

I was much disturbed and began to pour out my heart, telling the priest what had been happening and about my inability to understand. He listened, then we discussed the situation. Near the conclusion of our talk he said, "Did you ever ask God to work His will in your life?" I said, "Yes, in Alcoholics Anonymous it is one of the Steps of the Program." He said, "Well, it seems to me that God has started to take your life apart and rebuild it." His remark made me consciously aware for the first time of the significance of the events that were taking place in my life and it gave me fresh insight into my new adventure.

Not too long afterwards I returned to Columbus, Ohio. At that time I prayed to God, telling Him that I didn't know where He was leading me or what I would be doing, but I had obligations that I had to fulfill. I asked Him then to provide me with good health so that I might be able to fulfill those obligations. The obligations primarily centered around providing financial support for my four minor children yet at home. I not only vividly recall having prayed that prayer, but I also recall its coming back to my remembrance many times. I looked back and saw how God had removed some of the past afflictions from my body and how He had kept me. Even then, prior to consciously and publicly accepting Christ as my Saviour, God began to work in my life and teach me.

In that particular phase I became aware that when my faith weakened and I gave up in discouragement, the Lord would save the situation. I began to feel contrition about my failures of faith and it also seemed to be taking a little longer to get over them. Prior to that time, it really didn't matter much, but it soon became evident to me that I must trust God and walk closer to Him.

Having lost my job after nearly eighteen years, I unsuccessfully looked for work, and within the following week, I was headed for a financial crisis.

One evening I walked into my apartment, sat in my big easy chair and just flat out said, "Lord, I have prayed as much as I can pray. I have told you all my problems. I have told you all my needs. You know all there is to know about me—I just ain't going to pray anymore. Won't you please help me already?" I barely finished that prayer when the telephone rang. I half-heartedly dropped my hand to the table, adjacent to the chair, raised the phone and said, "Hello." The voice on the other end informed me that my resume had been reviewed, and I was accepted for a design position in Texas.

After I hung up the phone, all I could do was weep in thanksgiving and repentance, because again I had held out till the very end and then had thrown in the towel just prior to the time the Lord had reached out to help me. I went through subsequent situations like that because the Lord was teaching me the endurance (obedience and faith) that would be required in my new adventure.

I shared this incident with my close friends in A.A., finding security and sobriety through this. They shared my happiness in seeking God through meditation, praying for knowledge of His will and the power to carry that out. I had an improved conscious contact with God.

Hired by a Texas firm, I was sent back to the Los Angeles area on a temporary assignment, where I resided in Torrance and worked in Burbank. It was 1970 when I left Los Angeles and moved to the Dallas area. In Dallas I heard the plan of salvation for the first time, realizing more things God had been doing in my life. I became grateful for His work through my alcoholism and in my ongoing sobriety.

I THREW THE HORSE

It wasn't long till God produced, what I consider to be, major manifestations in my life. I began attending Full Gospel Businessmen's Fellowship Meetings in Dallas and heard testimonies of people being healed, among other miracles occurring in their lives. I began to realize that past physical afflictions were leaving me.

In preceding years, I had been put on thyroid medication by a doctor in Ohio who believed I would have to take it for the rest of my life. Although I didn't like the thoughts of an ongoing temporary remedy, I did not feel I had much choice. Fortunately, God does not abide by man's laws or what doctors say. "Testing God," I was impressed to reduce the thyroid medication slowly, hoping to cease taking it at all. With reduced applications, I found no ill effects. In prior times without the medication, I had undergone severe spells of tiredness, sleepiness, and a lack of energy. Subsequently I was feeling none of those symptoms and was impressed to flush the medication down the toilet, which I did.

On a Saturday, while visiting friends in the Grapevine area north of Dallas, I took to riding a temperamental beast of a horse. Being just as temperamental as he, we ended up in a conflict of minds—on the ground. There is a standing controversy about this when some refer to the incident as the horse's having thrown me.

The incident went like this: The horse started to buck and rear, and I pulled hard on the reigns to keep his head up because I was determined to have my way. So he let me have it. He stood up on his hind legs; then when I thought he would settle back to the ground, he settled on his haunches, and rolled to the side over my right leg, causing my head to whiplash into the ground. Although I got the worst of it, I was the "winner." To this day I say, "I threw the horse!"

The following Monday at work, however, I began to have dizzy spells and feared that I may have suffered internal damages. Two days were spent in a hospital undergoing observations and tests.

The doctor was afraid that there might be a broken bone in the sinus area because of the pain I was experiencing below my right eye, which radiated down into the upper gums. He was contemplating surgery, but final consideration of the tests and X-rays determined that there was only temporary nerve damage in the cheek. My upper right teeth and gums were numb for a couple of weeks.

Prior to my release from the hospital, I questioned the doctor about the tests and their results. He informed me, among other things, that my thyroid check was normal. I shared with him that I had been on medication for a thyroid condition and had been informed that I would have to use that medication for the rest of my life. I said, however, that I had quit using the medication and was feeling fine. Upon my request, he re-ran the test. Three tests by two different methods showed a normal thyroid reading each time. I have not had the tired spells or need for the thyroid medication since.

As I look back over the years I realize that the increased conscious contact with God, the expectation of His move in my life, which was the building of faith and my increasing trust in Him, were the major factors that strengthened my line of communication with Him.

The days of spiritual laziness were behind me and the days of spiritual adventure had begun.

PHYSICAL THERAPY

Having had a boost in my faith as a result of the thyroid healing, there was renewed encouragement in seeking further things of God.

By this time I had bought my first Bible and had begun to get into the Word. The next thing that greatly impressed me happened during a visit to *Christ for the Nations* in the Oak Cliff District of Dallas.

Even after the thyroid healing, though, I was still a bit skeptical about what I was seeing. I was seated near the front of the audience where I could clearly see what was going on. There were several people who went to the front for various afflictions, such as partial loss of hearing, vision discrepancies, etc.

There was a call for a lady with a short leg to come forth, that she would be healed. A lady went to the front and sat down. The lady's legs were placed in a horizontal position on a chair. A man sat at her feet and touched her ankles while he prayed. I sat there and watched the lady's short leg grow approximately one inch! I might have been totally skeptical about that, except that I saw it and heard bones cracking in her body. It was not something that could be simulated. This was the first time that I had actually seen a physical change in a person's body when prayed for in the name of Jesus Christ.

At the same service, there was a handsome boy, approximately 12 years old, who had been stone deaf from birth. As the boy was prayed for in the name of Jesus Christ, I saw his countenance change and his eyes light up brilliantly as he ever so slightly heard the ticking of a wrist watch. I could hardly be skeptical about that, especially after seeing the large crowd of overjoyed people around this young man. I can still see the awe in his face as he heard for the first time. It was a heart-rending experience. Love radiated from the hearts of the people around him in compassion and then in joy.

I harbored minor skepticism for some time, because the lady had not jumped up and down, or acted at all like it was any kind of a big deal. I am not skeptical about it anymore because I have seen people healed many times since. When God healed me, I was joyful and thankful and shared it with other people. I did not react quite the way that I thought I would, nor the way I thought the lady with the short leg should have. But now I know that God is real. God does perform miracles, and to people who believe and receive healings from God, it is an everyday thing. Yet I know it is beyond the comprehension of the average person who has not experienced it.

SODOM AND GOMORRAH

I'd had considerable domestic difficulty and was nearly severed from my past. After taking the Third Step in the A.A. Program and spending hours seeking God on Redondo Beach, California, I entered into a new kind of spiritual battle.

I had reached a point of certain dissatisfaction, not only with man's religion but with the A.A. Program, and I knew that there was more to finding a simple way of life, with a greater reality of God.

After nearly forty years, I left the Catholic Church, and after arriving in Irving, Texas, I began attending Plymouth Park Baptist Church. I was still seeking. It was there that I first heard the plan of salvation and became aware of several things. I knew that I was saved, and that if I died, I was going to go to heaven. I knew that in crying out to God (as I understood Him) and Jesus Christ, turning my life and my will over to the care of God, while praying for His true concept, I had made a commitment and now I wanted to profess Christ before man. I realized that a certain fear of death was gone and that I had long since given up any concern about confessing my sins to a priest every Saturday night.

Shortly thereafter, I accepted Christ publicly, in the Baptist Church.

"The Spirit itself beareth witness with our spirit,
that we are the children of God." [89]

In the meantime the spiritual battles continued, with occasional thoughts of returning to the past. There was fear as to what was ahead if I deviated from the religious teachings of my earlier life.

I had been plagued with many problems, needing answers, as to what God would have me do. That's the way it was on a dingy morning in 1970. I hesitated in my preparation for work that morning and got down on my knees in prayer.

"Lord, make Yourself real to me! I want to know that You hear me! I want to know that it is You who is speaking to me!" For the first time in my life I *insisted* that God make Himself real to me. I persisted and persisted. The following events occurred in a very short period of time: I was resting my head in my hands and I was praying; I was looking into darkness, which immediately was being consumed by a fire. Great flames were licking up from burning rubble. I was standing on a shallow knoll overlooking a plain of destruction—the flaming remnants of a city of many years ago. As I looked out over this flaming debris, I could see to my left a figure standing motionless. It was a human form, to the extent that it was the height of a human body and the shape of a head and shoulders, clad in a long robe or shawl.

As rapidly as all this appeared, it disappeared. Although I had not heard any sound or audible voice, my mind was strongly and clearly impressed repeatedly with the words "obedience" and "faith." Needless to say, I was very much frightened. Almighty God had made Himself real to me by showing me the vision of something I felt that I had seen before, not knowing exactly where or exactly what. It definitely was of a Biblical nature, and it definitely was an answer to my prayer.

Needless to say, this was the beginning of a great adventure in which I came to know that God *is* real. God sees all and will speak to us just as He has spoken to man for thousands of years. I was awe stricken.

Later that morning, with the help of a Christian friend, I found that the vision the Lord had given me was a vision of Sodom and Gomorrah. In the following days I realized that God had directed me to obedience and faith in following my personal experience with Jesus Christ and not to look back or be concerned with the preceding years of man's religion.

The story of Sodom and Gomorrah is found in the first book of the Bible in Genesis 19. It is the story of Lot and his wife departing with their family from Sodom and Gomorrah upon notification, by angels, that the city was to be destroyed because of the homosexual rampage, among other sins.

"And Lot went out and spoke unto his sons-in-law
which married his daughters and said,
"Up, get you out of this place
for the Lord will destroy this city." [90]

"And it came to pass when they had brought them forth abroad
that he said, escape for thy life, look not behind thee,
neither stay thou in all the plain, escape to the mountain
lest thou be consumed." [91]

"Then the Lord rained upon Sodom and Gomorrah
brimstone and fire from the Lord out of heaven.
And he overthrew those cities and all the plain, and all

*the inhabitants of the cities,
and that which grew upon the ground."* [92]

The Scriptures define the figure in the vision as Lot's wife.

*"But his wife looked back from behind him
and she became a pillar of salt."* [93]

*"And he looked toward Sodom and Gomorrah and toward
all the land of the plain and beheld and lo
the smoke of the country
went up as the smoke of a furnace."* [94]

That morning I prayed; I desperately needed God to speak to me; I believed that He would hear me, and I was very shortly overwhelmed by the actual experience.

It is through diligent seeking that God grants grace that the seed of faith may grow to the point where it can be exercised.

The Lord considered my weaknesses, my inabilities and took into account my ignorance. He guided me and gave me what I needed.

The Word says that our Father will not turn us away.

*"All that the Father giveth me shall come to me; and him that
cometh to me I will in no wise cast out."* [95]

A NEW KIND OF DESERT

In November and December of 1970, as an aeronautical engineer, I was assigned to a project at Edwards Air Force Base (E.A.F.B.), which included my making trips from Dallas, Texas, to Burbank, California, and Lancaster, California. It was also a time of great spiritual quest.

The following is an experience that I had time and again during the weeks that I spent on the Edwards project.

Early in the morning, I would drive the usually traffic-free highway, across the Mojave Desert to the E.A.F.B. facility. As I left the city limits of Lancaster, alone with the Lord, I felt that he was bathing my soul in an abundant joy that I had never before experienced (even though I had begun to experience small moments of joy back in A.A.). It was a kind of joy, peace, and happiness, impossible for the human mind to describe. As I drove across the desert, tears fell from my eyes. I wept because I could not bear the overwhelming joy. I just wanted to see Jesus. I looked up at the beautiful bright sky, which was spotted with puffy white clouds and the morning sunshine. There was a dry lake bed, desert sand and the jutting rocks—a most beautiful experience. I had gone through trying times, having been alone for a couple of years, but I knew that God was with me.

I was experiencing this joy and peace because the Scripture had taken such a grip on my soul and my fellowship with the Lord was all consuming. I would drive out on the desert at lunch time or go to my car at coffee break time to read the Bible, rather than eat or have a cup of coffee. This closeness to God, through involvement in His Word, constituted fellowship with Him. This is what gives joy beyond containment, even when one is going through heart-rending trials.

On one particular morning as I drove across the desert, I was filled with such a tremendous joy that I lifted my eyes to the sky and yearned that God would open it, raise the other end of the highway into the clouds and let me drive right into heaven.

He routinely bathed me in overflowing joy and happiness in times of tribulation. It was an experience that only Jesus can give a person. This is my Saviour, Jesus Christ, the same Jesus who will be standing there with His hand outstretched on my "last" day. A taste of eternal divine happiness—that was such a blessed experience.

With my evenings spent "devouring" the Word, I had many other mornings of a very similar kind, but that particular morning I will never forget.

I had walked through the valley of death to sobriety, and God had comforted me.

"Yea, though I walk through the valley of the shadow of death,
I will fear no evil, for thou art with me.
Thy rod and thy staff they shall comfort me." [96]

The Lord brings me out and leads me into the abundant life of His joy and peace.

THE ROSICRUCIAN

Having prayed for spiritual guidance and God's true concept, I kept an open mind toward spiritual things and encountered several paths that deviated from Christianity and the Bible. The following experience is one that I had while staying in Lancaster during my E.A.F.B. assignment. It showed me how pervasive the occult is, that evil spirits exist and have bound some who will receive their reward of eternal damnation, if not freed from their bondage through Jesus Christ.

One evening, I sat in a coffee shop next to a man who appeared friendly, jovial, outgoing, and who apparently was somewhat acquainted with the waitresses. After sitting there for a while, we began to converse.

For a period of several weeks, I had become so engrossed in the Word that I spent hours each day studying Romans, Corinthians, Thessalonians and the like. The Lord was revealing so many things to me in the Word that I hungered for more and more.

Near the beginning of our conversation, which lasted three hours, I asked this man if his beliefs were of a Christian nature. At first he would not give me a straight answer, but by his hesitance, I knew he was not a Christian. He said he was a Rosicrucian. Before we got underway in our talk, I asked the Lord to cover me and protect me with the blood of Jesus Christ. I entered this "adventure" as a child of God, with complete peace and absolute assurance that no evil deception could overtake me.

This man believed in "free love," sex outside of marriage, and miracles. Every once in a while he would shudder as if he were cold, but when I inquired if he was, he said, "No," and went on talking.

He believed that another spirit could enter the human mind, when the person was "absent" by daydreaming or some other preoccupation. I am grateful for the security of the loving protection of God, my Father, in heaven. I wasn't about to buy any of what this man was selling. It would be a pretty sorry God I had, if he permitted evil spirits to possess me while I was perhaps daydreaming about my time with Jesus in heaven.

Also, the man made candles and gave them to people as gifts. He gave one to me and told me that if I would burn the candle while I was having sex with my girl friend (assuming that I did such things) that love would radiate throughout the room. The candle went into the garbage can.

He went on to tell me about his "love" experiences with his wife and other women. From the conversation, I learned that his wife had left him, accusing him of thwarting their child's mind with his spiritual practices. Naturally, he, being possessed, felt that his way of life was proper and that it portrayed a life of love.

At that time, by the grace of God, I was bestowed with a certain wisdom and knowledge. I was a babe in Christ, had very limited knowledge on how to contend with such a situation, and I give the Lord all the glory for "enlarging my steps under me so that my feet did not slip." I did not know anything about how to help the man or his family. What happened to this man or his family I do not know.

As far as his shuddering during the conversation was concerned, he informed me afterwards, that what he was trying to do was contact my spirit, convey to it and set up a relationship.

He asked me several times if I had felt anything. To this I simply and honestly answered, "Nope, I didn't feel a thing."

I praise God that He looks out for His babes and enlightens their minds when in a state of vulnerability. The person was put there by evil forces at that particular time to sway me the wrong way, rather than the true Christian way under the guidance of the Holy Spirit. I could have lived a life of intentional sin, under the guise of being a Christian. There is no telling how far my life could have gone in sin or what the extent of the damage might have been. I very well could have given myself to that so-called type of love, which is nothing more than fornication and adultery.

At this point I acknowledge the further goodness of God in that people in Texas were in intercessory prayer on my behalf, knowing I was sincerely searching for God. God protected me until I arrived, in His time, learning along the way what He wanted me to learn, perhaps for this book.

He Knows Before We Ask

I had an experience wherein the Lord showed me how He cares for us and how He knows our needs even before we ask.

In the fall of 1971 I had an accident while driving a tractor-trailer rig in Dallas. After leaving the trucking terminal with an improperly balanced load, on the first turn the truck—both tractor and trailer—turned over. Only on this particular day did I have a driving partner, whose injuries consisted of a concussion, while I suffered from bruised ribs and slight nose lacerations.

Since I had been badly shaken by the accident, in the days to come I went through considerable emotional stress. While driving my car to the freight company in the mornings, I worried about what the day might bring.

One day I hoped that rather than drive a truck (all the driving was within the city limits, which is the worst kind of driving), I would be transferred to work on the dock. That is what I was assigned for that day.

On another morning I felt that I would rather have one large load assigned to me, wherein I could drive to a destination and spend the day unloading, which would preclude the tensions of being in traffic. This was also exactly what I got.

Another day I was thinking I would prefer to work as a hostler in the yard rather than drive at all. Again, this was my assignment for that day. Days passed and I found that this was a daily "coincidence."

I had not consciously prayed or asked God to take care of me in this situation, but I knew that these were not just coincidences. Upon recognition of this, I thanked God and continued for several days observing how He would act according to my desires, without my even asking. It was a thrilling experience to know that God cares this much. It was thrilling to watch God meet my needs exactly as I had mentally expressed my desires.

After some time, I felt considerably stable and was able to see other good results from the accident. Looking back on how I had become accustomed, while in the trucking business, to driving my own truck during the preceding months, I realized that I had become somewhat careless. The accident was not a pleasant experience. But it was one of those things that taught me how God might deal with me while showing me His great love and mercy.

"Be not ye therefore like unto them for your father knoweth what things you have need of before you ask him." [97]

BYE-BYE, BURSITIS

Years ago, I was afflicted with bursitis in the shoulder. Eventually it spread to both my shoulders, then my hip. Warning pains started, usually at night, while lying on one side or the other. The pain would grow stronger for several days until it became so severe that I had to have injections to stop the pain. I would always hold out until that night, when I could not find comfort in any position and would whimper through the remainder of the night, waiting for day to come so I could get to the doctor.

In the summer of 1971, while in the trucking business, I lived in my truck for six months. On one occasion I had a severe attack of bursitis in my right shoulder. It followed the usual course and got so bad that I had to drive my truck with one arm, which did not last very long because it was almost impossible to shift gears. When the severest pain set in, I got to a physician and received injections of Novocaine® and cortisone. I also took a prescription for the next several days. On the first night after the injections, I laid in my sleeper with terrible pain and wept. I wanted to get out of the truck, but I couldn't move because of the tight quarters in the bunk and the intensity of the pain. Each time I tried to roll over, I would cry out in pain. After some time of lying there in pain, unable to raise help, I became exhausted and fell asleep. This was an indication of the ailment's nature and viciousness.

At the time I didn't know anything about appropriating divine healing. I was spiritually ignorant of one of the privileges afforded me by the power of the Resurrection of Jesus Christ.

I was much more concerned, I suppose, with my material welfare rather than my spiritual welfare. I was not aware of the fact,

"But rather seek ye the Kingdom of God:
and all these things shall be added unto you." [98]

I went along, learning more of the Word, continuing to "test" God by putting into practice some of the things He was teaching me.

It was during the year of 1972 in New Orleans that I had a very severe bursitis attack in my hip. I eventually got to that night where I had no rest. I ended up in the living room trying to get comfortable. It came to my mind that I should rebuke the pain and command it to be gone from me. I became angry because of the pain, and in my anger and suffering I repeatedly rebuked it, binding the enemy by the blood of Jesus Christ. I commanded the enemy to cease his work on my body and depart. I was so weary and tired, so fatigued from fighting the pain. In addition to rebuking, I asked the Lord to grant me relief from the terrible pain. And this He did! Much to my amazement, the muscles relaxed in my hip and leg. I felt a complete subsiding of the pain. It was gone! I got up. I walked around. I simply enjoyed breathing during the great relief from the pain. After I walked across the living room several times, I laid on the couch and fell asleep. For approximately one hour, I had no pain. This had never happened before. Within that hour I gained enough strength to endure the night and get to the doctor the next day.

I was finding out about the power that Christ makes available to us. There were many things that I did not know, but I was learning. I still was not experiencing complete healing.

In the following months, I began to study about God's will in the Christian life and positive confession. It included the claim of divine healing and the clinging to it, despite pain symptoms, by professing positively with the mouth until the victory was achieved. Study on these subjects went on for several months and my faith was strengthened. God-given grace increased my faith to the point that in January of 1973 I claimed healing for the bursitis that I was quietly suffering in my left shoulder. As I went along, the Lord provided more study materials.

On a Saturday in March of 1973, I spent several hours studying divine healing in the Word, including James 5. During a period of three months, I continued without fail, to the best of my ability, to claim my healing, thanking God for it. I confessed positively that I had been healed.

During that time I went through trials of pain, discomfort, and loss of sleep, but I did not have a severe attack and did not require any medical attention.

I selected the prerequisites for healing, meditated upon them and had them fixed in my mind.

"Is any among you afflicted? Let him pray. Is any merry?
Let him sing psalms. Is any sick among you?
Let him call for the elders of the church;
and let them pray over him,
anointing him with oil in the name of the Lord:
And the prayer of faith shall save the sick,

and the Lord shall raise him up;
and if he have committed sins, they shall be forgiven him." [99]

It is not by coincidence that the Sunday School lesson the next morning was on divine healing. Neither was it a coincidence that the teacher deviated from the routine at the end of the Sunday School lesson. He announced that a healing line be formed and anyone who needed healing should step forth. By this time I had my Bible open to James 5. I raised up out of my seat with my Bible open, silently saying, "Lord, I know you have healed me, and I am going for complete victory."

I was anxious for an opportunity to raise my hand to inquire about the anointing with oil, as stated in the Scripture. I wanted to make sure that it was done right, or I wanted to know why anointing with oil would not be done. It was no coincidence either, that from the back of the church the minister announced that he had been led to bring the anointing oil, because he felt that it would be needed.

With each of these events occurring, I was highly elated and my faith was soaring because everything was falling into place. God was with me each step of the way, knowing my desires and needs. He knew how to teach me and provide for me. I had become hungry for knowledge of the Word and was hungry to experience further manifestation of God's power in my life.

I got into the healing line that Sunday morning and took my turn for prayer. Men of the church laid their hands on me, prayed the prayer of faith, and anointed me with oil, but I felt nothing at that particular moment. Within five minutes after returning to my seat, I felt a relaxing of the muscles in my shoulder, a rising sensation of warmth in the arm, then all the pain left.

Previously, I had reached a point of pain unlike any other within the three-month period. The pain was so severe, Sunday night would have been the night of weeping, waiting for Monday morning to get to the doctor for an injection. I had strenuously and positively confessed during that three months, in the Word, close to God and was on the brink of having to go to a doctor. But I was healed by the hand of God, by exercising His Word.

Just as the lady in Dallas, at Christ for the Nations, did not bolt out of her seat, or jump up and down, I likewise remained quiet. In the following days I began to share my healing with other people, mostly Christians as I remember. I walked softly, claiming that I had been healed because I knew that God had touched me. The pain was gone and my arm was feeling better all the time. In a couple of days I could whirl my arm around as if it had never been afflicted.

Then I remember thinking that I had stood up for complete victory for my left shoulder. That had been the initial and primary source of my affliction. I had claimed healing just for it. So then, I claimed healing of bursitis for my entire body. I asked the Lord to heal all my joints—my shoulders, hips, any other part that might be afflicted, and began to confess that not only had my shoulder been healed, but I had been healed of bursitis—period.

I received my healing and complete victory over bursitis in March of 1973 and I was healed by the blood of Jesus Christ. My faith really received a "shot in the arm" that day. There were a few times when I had slight pains, but I quickly rebuked them. As I write, there have been twenty-five, bursitis pain-free years.

Even though I sought God, prayed, studied the Word, and confessed positively, internally I had some misgivings that made me wonder. With the grace that God gave me, I exercised faith to the uttermost, within my frail self; and He honored that, for which I am grateful.

There are emergency situations where scriptural prerequisites for healing cannot be met. This is part of the liberty in Christ. By faith, we can take command or control over the situation and be victorious by pleading the blood of Jesus Christ.

HE IS ABLE

After my initial Dallas experiences with Christ in 1970, I moved to New Orleans, Louisiana, and lived there from 1971 to 1975. My heart was heavy for my immediate family because of my separation from them and because I knew that their destiny was also to be united with all things under Jesus. I had many times when I sought God, anxious for the welfare of their souls. Quite often being impressed to pray for them, I felt as if I carried a grave burden.

One night in 1972 I was awakened by the weight of this burden and was so distressed, that I went to the kitchen, set my Bible on the table before me and prayed.

I read the Bible and the following words became authentic to me as I felt great release and victory!

"And they said, Believe on the Lord Jesus Christ, and thou shalt be saved, and thy house." [100]

I was given the assurance that the Lord would keep and save my household. This was a blessed occasion for me as I wept and thanked God.

At that moment I was released from all the anxiety, heartache, and pressure that had reached a high point after weeks of intense accumulation. Once I was able to contain myself, after this release and blessing, I turned the pages in the Bible and my eyes fell on another Scripture.

"And it was the third hour..." [101]

I looked at the clock on the wall. It was three o'clock.

This is one of the ways in which God has communicated with me. And it is the kind of a thing that only can happen between God and the Christian, with witness in the spirit. I had no further difficulties with this problem plaguing me, or robbing me of sleep. From that moment I have had peace about the matter.

> *"...for I know whom I have believed,*
> *and I am persuaded that he is able to keep that which*
> *I have committed unto him against that day."* [102]

At the time I did not know that "the third hour" was not three o'clock. Nevertheless, the Lord used it as confirmation and to build my faith.

I continue to praise God and thank Him for the work He is doing.

Each time I am impressed to pray for a member of my family, I ask God to do whatever is required at the particular time to turn that soul to Jesus. At times I receive word of an event in one of their lives which I know is God moving in response to my intercession. God's almighty love has displaced the enemy's works of fear.

As years go by, I am finding that God's salvation is being manifested in the lives of the children, and their mother. I am trusting God to complete the job.

During that same time period, I claimed all my family for eternal life with Jesus Christ, including my parents and brothers.

On a Sunday afternoon in 1973, I wrote a thirty-two page testimony to my parents, sharing what the Lord had been doing in my life during the years after I had left Pennsylvania in 1952. I sent the letter along with a large-print Bible and *Four Spiritual Laws* [from *Campus Crusade for Christ*].

Mother called me on Thanksgiving Day of 1974 and told me that she had asked Jesus to come into her heart "just like it says in the little book you sent," (the Four Spiritual Laws).

The *Four Spiritual Laws* is a small booklet that provides Scriptural guidance for sharing salvation through Jesus Christ. It is one of the most effective tools available and should be a part of every Christian's witnessing kit.

In 1976 I traveled to Pennsylvania to attend a surprise celebration of my parents' fiftieth wedding anniversary. On the evening of their anniversary, Dad knelt with Mother and me and asked Jesus to come into his heart. In 1979, Mom, at age seventy-three, went to be with Jesus. Dad received comfort from I Thessalonians 4:15-18, until in 1983, at the age of eighty-four, he also went to be with Jesus.

"For this we say unto you by the word of the Lord,
that we which are alive and remain unto the
coming of the Lord shall not prevent them which are asleep.
For the Lord himself shall descend from heaven with a shout,
with the voice of the archangel, and with the trump of God:
and the dead in Christ shall rise first: Then we which are alive
and remain shall be caught up together with them in the clouds,
to meet the Lord in the air; and so shall we ever be with the Lord.
Wherefore comfort one another with these words." [103]

I give praise and thanks to God for His faithfulness, especially that my parents accepted the Lord, through the Word, as did others in the family.

I'm still receiving letters from family members after hours of writing to, or sharing with them one-on-one, those who are experiencing God and are being freed from religious mediocrity. Some have taken more than twenty years to respond since my initial witnessing, while others are yet to come. I have the assurance that He is able and He is faithful. God's message is: "Ask, intercede in prayer and rest in faith."

PENTECOST SUNDAY

While in Dallas, during the period from 1970 to 1971, I attended Full Gospel Businessmen's Fellowship Meetings, and on several occasions "sought" the infilling of the baptism of the Holy Spirit.

I knew little about the baptism except that it was of a closer walk and part of the deeper life.

In October 1971 while driving trucks and working the freight docks in Dallas, I was called for a job interview in New Orleans, Louisiana.

In the mornings, prior to calling the freight companies to inquire about available work for the day, I would read the Word and pray. On a particular morning I addressed the Lord about a job in New Orleans and asked Him to tell me what His will was in the matter (to *stay* or *go*). I asked Him to answer me through the Word and as I opened the Bible, I added..."and please let it be in your own words." When I opened the red-letter edition, which was the only Bible I had, the following Scriptures stood out. They were the only words of Christ on the two pages.

*"And he said unto them, Go ye into all the world,
and preach the gospel to every creature. He that believeth
and is baptized shall be saved; but he that believeth not
shall be damned. And these signs shall follow them that believe:
In my name shall they cast out devils;
They shall take up serpents;*

and if they drink any deadly thing, it shall not hurt them;
they shall lay hands on the sick, and they shall recover." [104]

It was settled as the Lord had gripped my heart with the spiritual witness!

I do not advocate using the Holy Bible as a "Ouija" board, and found, as I grew in the Lord, that He doesn't either. The Lord does however, by the Spirit, give direction with spiritual witness, through the Word.

Upon arriving in New Orleans, spiritual satisfaction could not be found in any of the churches I attended during the first few months. I was fed up with "religion" and wanted more of the reality of Jesus Christ. Being led to the First Assembly of God Church, I heard what I had been seeking, which, in effect was, "I don't care what you are—Catholic, Baptist, Lutheran, etc. We don't ask you to join our church. We just invite you to come and worship Jesus Christ."

In the first six months, the Sunday School lessons were about the baptism and the works of the Holy Spirit. I feel that I received more of the "real thing" in that six months than in all my spiritual training prior to that time.

In the following months my spiritual training included further teaching about the work of the Holy Spirit, the observation of the operation of the gifts and the manifestation of God's power in my life, such as my bursitis healing.

My promise had been given in Mark 16:15-18 and I got down to serious business. My witnessing of Jesus and His gospel became an everyday thing. I was baptized by immersion in accordance with the command and motive of repentance and the remission of sins.

Several times I went to the altar to receive infilling of the Holy Spirit, as I had seen others do, but did not receive the evidence of tongues. Later, I confessed, "Yes, I received the baptism but I just don't have the evidence yet."

On Sunday, June 23, 1974, having arrived home from church, I went to the prayer closet. "Lord, I've got to have the evidence and I've got to have it now." I reviewed my study texts on how to receive the baptism and prayed, only to discover that I was convicted of pride. The Lord and I transacted over some of my shortcomings, and I gave them to Him the best I that I knew how.

For seven months my lips, tongue, jaw and vocal chords quivered at times during prayer and worship before I realized that I just had not released them to the Holy Spirit. There also had been "peculiar" syllables repeatedly going through my mind. I decided, after praying and asking the Lord to give me the evidence, that I would do my best to release my speech organs and repeat those syllables again and again.

I proceeded in that manner until I began to feel ridiculous and decided that I was going to quit. Then, Praise God, it was my "Pentecost Sunday." The Holy Spirit took over from deep down inside me and the "Living Waters" began to flow. My hands went up to the Lord, shaking, and all my speech organs were on automatic as the heavenly language flowed for several minutes. I had received the baptism in the Holy Spirit with evidence of speaking in tongues!

Many spiritual events occurred prior to my receiving the baptism in the Holy Spirit, including minor manifestations of the gifts of knowledge, healing, etc., but now many greater things were happening. Since the baptism, the Bible is a whole new book to me. By that I mean that new understanding and revelation are mine through the Holy Spirit, which has been borne out by the same experience of others.

On numerous occasions the Holy Spirit has spoken to my heart through impressions on my mind. When this happens, the following events take place: my thought process is stopped in the middle of whatever it's doing. There is a quietness that commands my attention, then I am impressed with God's communication.

One Saturday, all my thought activity was suddenly stopped and I was impressed strongly to pray for "our" old church building, which had not been sold and lay unoccupied. I had been working on my auto, not thinking about the build-ing, when I was impressed to pray, particularly in respect to vandalism, which I did. The following morning I sat in church and listened to the announcement that the old church had been vandalized on the preceding day. God was strengthening my line of communication.

One week later, I was doing carpenter work for a minister friend, building a wall to partition a large room of a dorm for a storage area on one side and his daughter's room on the other. Without much ado, we had agreed on how to do the job.

I was working alone on Saturday, when I reached the end of the wall where the door was to go. All thought activity again stopped and I stood quietly, waiting! Then I was over-whelmed with concern, compassion and love for the daughter, of whom I knew very little. This did not originate from myself because there were no personal grounds for it, but the feeling of love so gripped me that tears fell down my face and I knew that it came from God.

Many things went through my mind about the room arrangement and the fact that others, outside of their family, would have to go through the daughter's room to reach the storage area, leaving her privacy interrupted. As a result, I changed the plans and joggled the wall at the door location to insure total privacy.

The following morning at church, I told the mother how I had changed the plans. Her eyes opened as large as quarters and her mouth dropped as she said, "Why did you do that?" Being half afraid to tell of my experience, I said, "I just thought it would be better." Then she told me how she had sought God and prayed all Saturday afternoon about her concern for the daughter's privacy. All the things that she told me were the same things that had gone through my mind the day before when the Lord had spoken to my heart—in answer to her prayers! Then I told her what really happened, because it was now confirmed. We both received a great blessing of God's love and concern.

Among the gifts of the Spirit that may operate in a Christian's life is the gift of healing.

For several weeks the words had been going through my mind, "Preach *and* confirm".... "Preach *and* confirm." I kept saying, "Who? Me, Lord?" Again and again..."Preach and confirm." I was being impressed to minister healing, but I kept shying away from it because there was the fear again...." You might make a fool of yourself." "What if the Lord lets you down?" The enemy is always in there, trying.

On a Wednesday night I prayed before going to bed, asking the Lord to bring a larger harvest of souls to a commitment to Jesus. I had been faithful in the witnessing of Jesus to others, sharing in His wondrous works and salvation, and I wanted to see more people realize the great love of Christ.

The following morning I was led to a lady whose husband had been diagnosed with terminal cancer. He had five tumors in his lymph nodes and one internal malignancy. Talk about a growth challenge! The same message: "Preach *and* confirm."

"Is anything too hard for the Lord?" [105]

The next week or two included hours of prayer and walking easy with the Spirit. Each step was taken slowly and as spiritual witness was felt. The man accepted the Lord on our first encounter. I fasted and continued to pray for faith to grow in all involved. I prayed for the Lord to release him from the hospital and after a couple more days, I took his hand, rebuked the enemy and the cancers, and asked the Lord to heal him in the name of Jesus, by His precious blood—the power of the Resurrection.

We prayed according to the man's desire, for him to be released from the hospital. Minutes afterward, one of his doctors walked into the room and said he could go home the next day. Tests had shown that the five lymph node tumors had disappeared and that his blood count had returned to normal. He returned to work with new hope in life.

In addition, the Lord brought at least seven other members of the family and relatives to a commitment to Jesus, and the harvest persisted as the Lord continued to hear prayers.

The remaining internal malignancy eventually took the man's life despite our support of his battle. He had been given six months to a year to live but remained with us for two years. About three months before his death, I knew he had given up the battle. When we prayed positively and pled the blood of Jesus, he responded with new faith and health. Finally, when the battle became too difficult, he wanted to be taken to be with the Lord. It became evident that he had given up the battle.

"My people are destroyed for lack of knowledge," [106]

It is very difficult for one to rise up with sufficient faith for victory during a "terminal" illness, especially when they have not been grounded in the Word of God.

I received the same Scripture (loud and clear) when I got the news that the man had died.

Testimonies have been given in other such cases where the person knew it was his time to go, and he went with total joy and peace.

Others have been totally victorious in defeating cancer and other terminal illnesses by application of the Word.

Many come to the Lord late in life and late in the knowledge to face the tribulations that come upon them.

Note that my original prayer was for more souls to make a commitment to Jesus and His great love. The Lord extended the man's life from six months to two years, gave him, and a harvest of his loved ones, the greatest gift—eternal life with Jesus Christ.

Our natural desires are for the body and this life, but, although we find it difficult to understand, God's desire is far greater.

Since this experience, the Lord has privileged me to minister other healings.

A young man of seventeen with rheumatic fever, healed—which included previous "permanent" damage from his younger years; and a young man of approximately twenty-two years with a concussion, severe pain and possible kidney damage. I prayed for him at 6:30 in the evening at the hospital and he called me from home at 9:00 the next morning. He was completely healed, after a painless, sleep-filled night.

There have been others who were healed, all of whom first accepted Christ and asked Him to take the throne of their life. However, people are often converted after receiving God's merciful healings.

As one learns the "voice of the Spirit," one must also learn the "check of the Spirit." I have become overly-anxious at times and in particular circumstances have been physically checked from acting.

I know that it is not due to our merits that the healings come, but because of the work that God wants done in our lives. I feel that conditions must be met, not only by the person who prays, but also by those who are prayed for.

Please understand that I am not trying to impress anyone that a person must have the Pentecost experience with the evidence of tongues to be saved, to receive the Holy Spirit or pray for the sick. My desire is to share the route I have traveled and encourage others to seek Jesus, not the "things." No one has ever "figured out" God or ever will.

A Fiery Exchange

In March of 1978, I rented an apartment in Bellevue, Washington, which was on the top floor of a three-story apartment complex that housed approximately 200 people.

Upon entering the apartment building for the first time, I felt very strong impressions of spiritual oppression in the building. It felt as though demons were running up and down the corridors. I remember thinking that I didn't want to live there, but I was impressed that God wanted to do some work of which I was to be a part. The issue was settled, as I realized this was to be part of my new adventure in Christ, thinking it would probably be consummated in daily witnessing to people. I never thought it would include anything like bailing out of a burning building in the middle of the night and being forever separated from all the material treasures of this life. These treasures included such items as school medals, photos, and other irreplaceable memorabilia.

Shortly after moving into the apartment, I was impressed to get a rope to use as a fire escape, which I did. Living there for seven months, I often thought about how I would get out if there should be a fire. It was as though God was putting me through a mental rehearsal for a coming event. Since I was alone, I planned on getting just myself out of the building, along with a metal box containing personal documents. I lived in a corner apartment and had the option of escaping to the north from my living room or to the west from my bedroom. I planned to tie the rope to the handle of the sliding door in the living room and I would go down each successive balcony to the ground. The alternate was to tie the rope to the bathroom door hinge and exit out the adjacent bedroom window.

My prayer life consisted of many hours spent on my knees at my desk. One of my prayers, prior to the fire, was a re-dedication to the Lord of myself and all that I "owned." Also included in that prayer was a plea to the effect that he would accept these things in exchange for a great testimony unto Him. My communication with God was really remarkable, because I was learning to 'trust in the Lord with all my heart, lean not unto my own understanding, and He was directing my ways.'

One Wednesday evening, upon arriving at home from work, my thoughts were abruptly put on hold, and I was impressed that the apartment building was going to be burned by an arsonist. Then I was shown the face of the man who lived in the apartment just a few doors from mine.

Although God had communicated with me before, I did not feel led (or bold enough) to share these impressions with anyone else, and I retired as on any other evening.

Since then, I have thought how powerful it would have been for me to have shared this "word of knowledge" and been found by everyone to have some special powers given by God. All power, however, is Christ's, which is given by God.

"And Jesus came and spake unto them, saying,
All power is given unto me in heaven and in earth." [107]

We can exercise our God-given power for good or evil. The working of God's power through us is not under our control, but we can choose to be God's instrument for His use, according to His purpose. Doing mechanical things to be a miracle worker is not possible with God.

I realize now that's one of the shortcomings of religion and of man. Teaching people to obtain power and become a great evangelist for God has been a strong flowing theme, often overdone, in religion. Learning to pray, receive power from God, and yet be flexible enough in His hands to have Him perform His will is apparently too much of a temptation for most people. For me, it is taking a long time to learn to maintain that devotion and flexibility. I have long since stopped saying, "God told me—." The further I walk as a Christian, the more reluctant I am to accept those words when I hear them spoken. I feel much more comfortable, peaceful and serene in letting the Lord God Almighty do what He will, period. Even though I pray that God will be glorified, and that I will not seek self-glorification, I have to admit that I occasionally (usually with hindsight) catch a glimpse of that desire, regardless of my determination. I praise God for all that He has done in my life and for all that He has undone to keep me from self-seeking.

A local newspaper referred to the Thursday, October 5, 1978 fire as "the 1:32 AM blaze, the worst in city history." As I recall, I was asleep in the burning building for about forty minutes. At that time, none of the apartments in the complex had smoke detectors or sprinklers. I was awakened by what sounded like someone pounding on the walls or running in the building. There was screaming from the adjacent apartment, "How do I get out?" and "Which way do I go?" Sitting up, I found the apartment filled with smoke. I got out of bed, having to stoop down because the upper air space was so thick with smoke. Not being able to see very well, I walked to the adjacent hall and looked into my living room. Everything was brightly lit outside the sliding glass doors of my living room balcony and I knew that the building's roof was ablaze over me. Then I became aware of the crackle and popping sound of burning wood, as in a freshly lit fireplace, which was coming from just outside my apartment door in the corridor. I knew enough not to open the door if I wanted to survive. At that time I became awake enough to realize that, "My God, this really is happening!"

I returned to my bedroom and automatically put the egress plan into action. Having on a T-shirt and shorts, I put on a pair of trousers and shoes. The next thing I did was to drop the metal box out of the window, take the rope that I had stowed in my bedroom closet, tie it to the bathroom door's lower hinge, and drop the loose end out the bedroom window. I then realized that it was cold outside and went back to the closet to put on a jacket. At some point I also put on a pair of gloves to protect my hands thinking it would be rough to go down the rope with my bare hands. Then I straddled the windowsill and wrapped the rope around one of my hands. The rope was made of slippery nylon, but I never thought to put knots in it a couple of feet apart. I slid out the window, dragging my left leg across the sill as I went out, momentarily hanging there until I twisted my hand free from the rope. When I did that, I went down, literally, "like a shot!" Except for the friction of my gloved hands on the rope, nothing slowed me down until I hit the ground. The gloves had neat grooves burned in them, and so did my hands which were rope burned and a little bloody. I also must have hit a protruding vent on the way down, or a shrub when I hit the ground, because later I discovered that one of my shins was bleeding too. The next day, I found a purple bruise that ran down the length of the inside of my left leg where I had dragged it across the windowsill on egress.

As a fireman and I approached each other, he asked me where I had come from and I pointed up to the window of my apartment. He asked me how I had gotten out and I pointed to the rope, which was still hanging from the window. At that moment, the lady in the apartment next to mine was at her window, screaming for help. The fireman told her to hang on and not to jump, that he would get her down, which he did, by ladder.

The rest of the night was spent watching the activity of this three-alarm fire. There was a little guy, wrapped in a blanket, with only trousers and shoes on, whom I kept with me for a while because he seemed to be more in shock than most others from the fire. Later we received comfort from the Red Cross and the church next door.

As I looked up to my apartment, I saw that the burning balcony railing was hanging haphazardly and the living room's sliding glass doors had been blown out. The roof was gone, and it appeared that the fire balls were rolling in from above and out through the door opening. Swirling waves of flame consumed my apartment and all my worldly life-time treasures. People had been jumping from windows and others were breaking out windows and tying blankets and sheets together in an attempt to get out of the building. I saw a fireman barely escape having a large blazing piece of the building front fall on him as he was coming out of the building. I was approaching the building from across the street, and because of my state of shock, I could not yell at the fireman. Fortunately, there was a fireman walking behind me who yelled and signaled the fireman who was in jeopardy to jump back into the building and out of the way. It was a night I will never forget and never want to experience again. One such fire in a lifetime is too much, considering all the trauma associated with it.

Within hours of the fire the police arrested the man, whose face I had seen on the eve of the fire, and another man, both of whom had lived in the apartments.

On the following Sunday, three days later, the third floor tenants were permitted back into the building. In shock and awe I went back to the area where my apartment had been, just to look and take photos. There were the bed springs, all that was left of the bed in which I had been sleeping. Metal remnants of my dining set, typewriter, phonograph turntable, and other items lay twisted and blackened. My apartment had about six inches of black ashes and muck on the floor. This was my new furniture and all of my material possessions. All I had left was my automobile.

A couple of days after the fire, as I was having breakfast with the pastor of the church I had been attending, I came to a realization. I looked at the pastor and said, "Jack, the manuscript is gone!" The manuscript first cut for this book had been completed two years earlier and was being rewritten. After two years of work on the manuscript, I had a hard time accepting the fact that it had been destroyed. The thought was nearly unbearable for I could not understand why God would let the manuscript be destroyed when it was part of my Christian testimony that I was so eager to share.

On that Sunday as I probed the ashes, I dug in a corner near the floor where I had stored one copy of the manuscript and found it, sandwiched between a couple of hard plastic binders. I wept as I found it intact, except for the *upper* part of the pages which had been burned away. At least I had something to work with in putting it back together. It occurred to me that I had stored another copy of the manuscript on the lower shelf of a hall closet. As I probed this area, I found the stationary box containing it, protected by some other thick book materials. It was a miracle that the entire closet was burned to ashes, including every shelf, except for the area holding the box. This copy I found to be intact except for the *lower* parts of the pages being burned away! At this point I was emotionally ecstatic. I raised my hands to heaven, wept and praised God for preserving the manuscript. He indeed had given me a testimony in fiery exchange for all the worldly possessions that I had dedicated to Him.

Fire officials were quoted in local newspapers as saying: "Many of the people in this fire did panic and act improperly because they didn't plan ahead", and "If they had been more prepared, there probably would have been fewer injuries." If God had not done my planning for me, I would not be here today.

Chapter Four

Winners Only

"I have kept the faith: henceforth there is laid up for me a crown of righteousness, which the Lord, the righteous judge, shall give me at that day: and not to me only, but unto all them also that love his appearing." [108]

NEW ADVENTURE – NEW LIFE

Most of us believe in the beautiful story of the birth of the infant Jesus in Bethlehem. Some celebrate Christmas with very little mention of Him, concentrating instead on the abundance of material goods.

Looking at only the worldly aspects, one hinders capabilities of growth and never realizes the true meaning of God and the fullness of His fellowship. Let us look beyond celebrating Christmas in the material aspects, and take the rest of the story through to the ugly crucifixion of this same Jesus. The Bible is the historical account of His walk on Earth, as well as His birth, and a whole new life in the power of His Resurrection.

Swept away with material things, one can never grow or learn until taught discipline. When God is put first, one will have the proper relationship with others and self.

It is not only God's will, plan, and desire, but it is our obligation to ourselves and our loved ones to look beyond and grow through dependence on God, trusting Him for guidance in all things.

It is very important to

*"Trust in the Lord with all thine heart;
and lean not unto thine own understanding. In all thy ways
acknowledge him, and he shall direct thy paths."* [109]

Herein we find the key to fulfillment sought in the Serenity Prayer.

The Serenity Prayer

God grant me the serenity
To accept the things I cannot change,
The courage to change the things I can,
And the wisdom to know the difference.

Our human mind prevents us (even with hindsight) from realizing precisely what God wants for our lives. Sometimes we are able to look back and see how God has worked through an utterly confused mess that we stumbled through. We can look back and see how God has neatly put the puzzle together despite our ideas and efforts in a situation. While we were going through the situation, we should have done things differently but still would not have achieved anywhere near the same goal. Many things have changed in my life, and I know that God changed them through Christ, not through any ability of mine. Some were pretty subtle. Others, I have yet to understand.

Learning the Word is important in seeking not a religion but Jesus Christ, and in receiving guidance through the Holy Spirit with the internal witness that lets one know what is right. Sometimes there are doubts about the internal confirmation because some inputs are not from God. These can be checked by the fruit of the Spirit and judged accordingly.

Seeking Christ and the guidance of the Holy Spirit through the Bible is our direct line to God, available twenty-four hours a day. Through the Word, we come to realize how insignificant, how little we are, and how imperfect our minds are compared to the almightiness of God. We begin to realize that if

God can enlighten our minds by His Holy Spirit, most assuredly He did enlighten the minds of those (so-called) "simple" people who contributed to writing the Bible.

People are sometimes misled because seemingly, "simple" ones go overboard in accepting Jesus Christ. God doesn't pick "great, self-made" people for His use. He takes the little ones and makes them "great." Great, self-made people don't want Jesus and are not made into usable people until they get to the foot of the cross, where the Lord can pick them up and begin to remold them. When people take up their crosses and humble themselves before God, only then can He begin the work. In the ensuing growth, people give the thrones of their lives to God, usually a little at a time, until they are led moment by moment by the Holy Spirit, and let God take control. Eventually, through the power of Jesus' Resurrection, those people are resurrected to eternal life and given their crowns, in everlasting fellowship with Him, according to their Spirit-led works on Earth.

I had little or no recognition of these "simple" people, but now I can listen to some of them on the radio, for instance, who preach the Word of God, and appreciate them. I know that many of these people have meager education or esteem in the eyes of the world.

Some of these people do not have the correct doctrine, which is only discernible by one's own knowledge of the Word and Spirit-led witness. Those who have the correct, Spirit-led doctrine are precious in the eyes of God and bring blessings to those who know the Lord.

The worldly, self-made person does not appreciate the Word of God or these "simple" people and continues in a life of self-will, sin, or perhaps worldly good works without faith in Jesus Christ. Christian principles will work, even in their lives, but they cannot attain heaven on their own merits.

"For they being ignorant of God's righteousness,
and going about to establish their own righteousness,
have not submitted themselves unto the righteousness of God." [110]

Some, out of curiosity, may pick up the Bible to see what they can understand, or what they might be able to accomplish with it. Little can be understood or accomplished until a commitment is made to Christ, asking Him to take the throne of their lives and, until they have a realization that we are all creatures of body, soul, and spirit.

It is through the spirit that the Word ministers to us. This is why a spiritual life is not the same as a religious life. For in religion we are doing things according to man's ways and accomplishing little. But in the spiritual realm, God is working through the Holy Spirit in us. This occurs where the Word applies and makes sense to those with a commitment to Christ. Only in this way can one receive direct revelations from God that can be supplemented with other devices.

Other devices are study materials, commentaries, various renditions of the Bible, concordances and such. A concordance is a book of the words in the Bible and the biblical passages where they can be found. Spiritual laziness is often enough to stop the quest for the treasures of God. Develop a determination to spend the time and effort to receive the blessings of an intimate fellowship with Jesus. Guides for purchase of supplemental materials can generally be obtained at Christian book stores and Christian churches.

God knows every situation and deals with people even before they make a commitment to Christ. God did not manifest Himself in my life nor did I have miracles working in my life until I accepted Christ as my Saviour. We cannot become a Christian by being born into a family that embraces a Christian Religion; each of us must consciously accept Christ of our own free will, which He will never overpower.

I do not believe that all people will go to hell if they do not worship as I worship. I do believe that if a person comes to repentance from a totally self-directed life, believes in Jesus Christ—that He walked the Earth as the Son of God, was crucified, and resurrected for our sins—he will go to heaven, unless he subsequently rejects Him.

*"For we are made partakers of Christ, if we hold
the beginning of our confidence steadfast unto the end."* [111]

Dependent upon the individual case and the sincerity of the heart, the Lord judges accordingly for He knows those who are His.

Appropriating salvation alone is not living the abundant life and becoming a "winner." There are Christians who consciously accept Christ but do not become winners in attaining the abundant life. This is due to a lack of seeking God, developing a conscious contact with Him, and seeking education through the Word.

Follow-up after accepting Christ is very important. For a Christian to stray from the Word is the same as enrolling for a college course then quitting after the first week. Certainly, little will have been achieved. So it is with accepting enrollment in the school of the Spirit toward gaining an abundant life and becoming a winner.

This is the reason why Christian fellowship is important, as recommended by some A.A. elements. To be a Christian is to be a part of the True Church Body, Jesus in the heart.

> *"For as the body is one, and hath many members, and all the members of that body, being many, are one body: so also is Christ."* [112]

A new Christian without follow-up instruction may fall by the wayside, but for the grace of God. Christian fellowship encourages growth and seeking, rather than waiting for God to take a hand. After I've prayed with someone to accept Jesus, on the byways of life (never to see them again here on Earth), I uphold them in prayer until I feel a release. I know God is faithful to carry on the work in that person's life.

The important thing to realize is that the True Church is not a building, a religion, organized group or denomination. All denominations do, for the most part, is to divide the Body. Your diligent, personal, one-on-one relationship with Jesus and the Word and with others who do likewise puts you in the True Church. Our ancestors came to America for freedom *of* religion, I wish they had come for freedom *from* religion. The body of Alcoholics Anonymous is more representative of a united repentant group than any religious group I have ever broached in my travel through most of the United States.

Accepting Christ starts a rebuilding process. All the things we feel we must do to survive are given to God to work out, and we in turn, yield to Him. We allow Him to work, showing by the Holy Spirit, all the things in our lives that are wrong; then we let Him remove them, one by one. This is something we can't grasp through reasoning and is one of those things that God makes real to us as we go along in the process.

A Christian would find it difficult to look to our Lord under the most severe, unhappy circumstances and not be able to say, "Thank you, Father, for Jesus and my salvation." It would be difficult for a Christian to dwell upon these things without receiving joy within the spirit.

I would like to tell all the world of my salvation liberties because they are something I have experienced, feel, and rejoice in, knowing that they are direct revelations from God through the Word.

Upon becoming a Christian, one receives the Holy Spirit, who guides and ministers to the Christian as the Christian yields. Through the baptism of the Holy Spirit, the Christian receives additional power to exercise the gifts of the Spirit, as God gives them to the individual according to His judgment.

"And there are diversities of operations, but it is the same God which worketh all in all. But the manifestation of the Spirit is given to every man to profit withal. For to one is given by the Spirit the word of wisdom; to another the word of knowledge by the same Spirit; to another faith by the same Spirit; to another the gifts of healing by the same Spirit; to another the working of miracles; to another discerning of spirits;

to another divers kinds of tongues:
But all these worketh that one and the self same Spirit,
dividing to every man severally as he will." [113]

The following recommendations are suggested for elevation to higher spiritual levels and the abundant life.

1. Pray daily and earnestly.
2. Complete faithfully a thorough initial repentance, and sustain an ongoing repentance such as outlined in the Twelve Steps of A.A.
3. Read and meditate on the Word of God (The Holy Bible) daily.
4. Consciously accept Christ and salvation and commit your life to Him.
5. Every moment of the day strive for obedience to the Holy Spirit.
6. Believe in the Word of God as His voice speaking to you.
7. Trust that the Lord is directing your every step.
8. Share with others what God is doing in your life.
9. Become a member of the true Church, Jesus in the heart.
10. Ask God to baptize you with the Baptism of the Holy Spirit.
11. Strive for the fruit of the Spirit in your life.
12. Confess only positive things in your life.

Each of the above is important for entering into a success-ful adventure in your new life of spiritual growth. Through the Word, you will learn all you need to know in your new rela-tionship with God, your fellowman, and yourself. You will also learn how to defeat the enemy.

Diligent application of the above will take you through many battles and certain victories, by the grace of God, and will make you an eternal winner.

We cannot be winners through materialism, religion or reli-gious inheritance, by trusting in ourselves, by looking to the "wise" people of the world, through feelings, or "phileo" (man's) love.

We can be winners through spiritual discipline, trusting God, the power of Christ's Resurrection, Christian fellowship, the full gospel, the Holy Spirit, prayer, repentance, faith, spiri-tual battles, and "agape" (God's) love.

Let it be known before you embark, that the life of a Christian is not a smooth, easy, painless, walk. It was not easy for Christ and cannot be easy for us. But more than that, know that it is a walk of promise, faith, and victory.

My drinking story is one of a person running from promise, faith, and victory, life and reality. Self-seeking in flesh-satisfying, material things—this was a life of a coward and a loser. The world does not satisfy with its "finality" in death.

If you have an unsatisfied feeling of spiritual immaturity (and you may be a regular churchgoer), God can be real to you if you will reach out through the full gospel. Many people are doing without the real experience because of reluctance to accept the full gospel. To me, this means believing all of the

Bible: the Old Testament and the New Testament including the gifts as described above in I Corinthians 12:6-11. It is not easy to accept full gospel worship because it goes beyond the usual limits of mankind's pride and lack of desire for the things of God. Humility, devotion and gratitude will get you there in time, if you truly seek God.

Everything doesn't end with the worldly death. Have the conviction of eternal life. Feel the victory as a Christian today; be a winner!

In the next section of this book, I relate more of my experiences showing how God is working in my life. Also, I review some of those items that constitute hang-ups to a commitment to Christ and growth in the Spirit. Included are recommendations on how to achieve new goals in spiritual growth.

SOLUTION TO ALL PROBLEMS

Having enrolled in the "School of the Holy Spirit," there are many things that I have learned and more that I will learn.

Prayer is one of these areas. My first prayers were memorized from a prayer book. To this I added prayers in my own words. Since I accepted Christ and enrolled in the school of the Holy Spirit, I have been given a new prayer life. Following my ministering to the Lord, I have a time of listening to the Lord. After this, I petition the Lord, in the name of Jesus, with a written list of people and causes for which I wish to pray.

Going further in the school, I was baptized in the Holy Spirit, as previously shared in "Pentecost Sunday." Now the Holy Spirit sometimes takes over certain items on my prayer list, places a burden beyond my personal burden, praying through me in tongues, according to God's will.

On my first attempt at my new prayer life of prolonged prayer, I prayed for two hours and was not ready to stop. God has continued to bless me with growth upon growth.

During these times of prayer, the Lord impresses me with direction and knowledge, which He confirms in the ensuing circumstances and works.

Praying in the Spirit relieves anxieties, fears, remorse, oppressions, and builds faith.

The Lord is receptive to our every desire and learning effort. When we seek, we do find. We must learn to do our part by exercising what He teaches us, by His Word and experiences—through grace. Negligence of the prayer life results in unrest and unsuccessful ministering.

Prayer with concurrent fasting has brought greater victories and joy of the Lord.

"...for the joy of the Lord is your strength." [114]

The spiritual life in Christ has proven to be the ongoing solution to all problems, for the joy and peace sought for my forty years as a religionist is now a growing reality!

Somewhere along the line, the Lord quickened the following Scripture to my heart and began to show me man's make-up:

"For the word of God is quick, and powerful,
and sharper than any two-edged sword, piercing even to
the dividing asunder of soul and spirit, and of the joints
and the marrow, and a discerner of the thoughts
and intents of the heart." [115]

I found that we are comprised of three components –

BODY: physical being–house of the soul and spirit (mortal)

SOUL: feelings, passions, desires (immortal)

SPIRIT: invisible force that knows, the mind (immortal)

This is an important realization to growth in the spiritual realm. Then we know that there is an invisible "being" to be dealt with, and it is through the spirit that the Holy Spirit deals with us.

As we grow in the spirit, we find that the "self" part of the body diminishes, and what is left is spiritually transformed, turns toward God. Upon further growth we find that we spend less time praying for ourselves and more time praying for others. We reach a place where we can trust God to take care of our needs while we devote more time to doing His will, in concern for others. We come to understand that the Scriptures point out spiritual poverty and point us to spiritual blessings, not only for ourselves but for other Christians, the Church, and the world in general. This results in concern for others, rather than just for ourselves and our own motives.

This kind of growth brings personal release from bondages due to self-importance and thereby solves many of our problems.

I point out some of these things to show the workings of the Holy Spirit, the true spiritual walk and growth which can come by no other power except through Christ and His Holy Spirit, considering any worthwhile, lasting value.

In writing this book, in obedience to God, I make part of my life known to others. It lets them know more about how I think and why, and what I am inside. It leaves my shortcomings open for evaluation by other people. They can pick me apart and try to reason out my attitudes and ideas. They will show their attitudes and differences of opinion to mine.

I'm happy for this opportunity because it is helping me to see myself as never before. It is a large step of growth because now I can meet these differences, evaluate them, learn from them, study my "peculiarities" and set new courses for growth.

Through writing this book, I have learned a lot about myself that needs correcting. It makes me realize that my righteousness through Jesus Christ is the only way to go, because I am mortally helpless and totally dependent on the promise of salvation as is evident in the Word and Jesus' walk to Calvary.

It also has shown me things about other people, because growth brings insight. I will continue to grow as long as I walk in the trust of God and keep an open mind and an open heart to the Holy Spirit. By meeting other's comments and opinions of my writings, I will be able to evaluate those people in return, by their rationale.

I am happy, for the grace of God, to be willing to admit my errors as the Holy Spirit reveals them to me through the Word, through other people, or directly, and thus, grow in Christ. I am sad because many people do not have the willingness of spirit, which goes beyond "head knowledge" and the willingness of the proud flesh.

It is sad; some are always "right" because they refuse to grow in the spirit. Even sadder is the fact that some of these people profess Christianity.

I'm going where Jesus is, and I've found that there is only one way to get there—the road to Calvary. Those who are not growing in the spirit are spectators behind the rocks along the road, who will not step out onto the bloodstained path with the others. They watch and dare not become one of them. Noted expressions of pride, fear, insecurity, etc., include the following:

"God made me the way I am, and He will change me when He is ready."

"If I step out there, people will really know what I am and will criticize me."

"If I join them and confess, then I will not be me (my self) anymore." ("I will have to be what God wants me to be.")

"I am so persecuted and mistreated already; I'll just stay here in the shelter of His arms."

"If I get out and help them, I wonder if they will help me."

"That's all right for people who need to feel persecuted."

"If I were honest with them, I might hurt their feelings."

"But I am committed to Christ!"

Some of these are not niceties. However, they are retorts or attitudes expressed in regard to God's Word, by Christians and non-Christians alike.

These things are part of my experiences and reflect what I have learned, heard, or lived myself. They are based on how God has worked in my life and the lives of others, and they are shared in the hope of helping others. I wish there was another way to tell some of these things, but the truth often hurts.

I will, as I go along, work at making the good things a part of my life, by the grace of God.

I've already paid a price to write this book—in falling short of the goal, in witnessing to others and finding out what to put in it—but then, I was bought with a price.

In the future, I will be criticized and even condemned by people; but in my walk with Christ, I know in whom I believe! And He is not dead, as the other so-called "gods" who are worshipped by those who refuse the risen, true God.

"And we know that the Son of God is come,
and hath given us an understanding, that we may know him
that is true, and we are in him that is true,
even in his Son Jesus Christ.
<u>This</u> is the <u>true</u> God, and eternal life." [116]

DIVINE HEALING

God receives glory through saving and healing.

When our healings occur, we want to tell everyone. But then we think, Who would believe us anyway? So we share with those who do believe. Others must see for themselves.

There is a big difference between hope and faith. People get desperate in time of need and cry out to God, hoping to be healed. Many times God honors these cries. Some of these people have not consciously accepted Christ, but God is merciful in drawing people by His Spirit. Without proper knowledge of the Word and spiritual education on how to appropriate divine healing, it is easy for a person to feel that there is no such thing.

Even with proper knowledge it is sometimes difficult to receive healing because of the hindrance of sin in one's life. This is not to imply that we receive anything from God through our own works. It means that sin weakens faith. I have been hindered in appropriating divine healings because I harbored resentments, or some other sins, and willfully refused to give them up or make amends for them. I have been impressed that I would not be healed of a specific ailment until such time as I relinquished that particular defect.

No one always knows what must be done to appropriate from God, but we know all things have been appropriated through the blood of Christ.

God expects us to strive, learn, and grow after we accept Christ. In heeding the Holy spirit and letting Him guide our lives, the Lord will strengthen us, make us new, renew our minds, and eliminate our defects and sins in His own way and time. It is up to us to follow His gracious lead, otherwise through ignorance we may fall victim to the enemy's afflictions.

In studying divine healing, my thoughts took me back to my old way of religious worship, when I was without a Bible and had little faith. Then my mind shifted to my present way of worship, with continuous guidance of the Holy Spirit, confirmation by miracles and other verifications through the Word.

> *"So then faith cometh by hearing,*
> *and hearing by the word of God."* [117]

God heals, but He does not mean to be an earthly fountain of youth. The Scripture plainly states that the body grows old. I believe that the Lord gives grace to claim healings when He is to be glorified.

Some of the tenderest testimonies have come from the lips of senior Christians who knew that the usefulness of their earthly body had ended and they were ready to go home to be with their maker.

Some have accepted only the promise of eternal life but never experienced such things as divine healing. They may live a life of one crisis after another, believing the Incarnation (life of Christ on Earth), but divine healing and the other thousands of promises are never claimed. There will be cases of divine healing, but without the real experiences and knowledge of the Word, the person cannot attain that place where they can consciously obtain further divine healing.

The Lord is very gracious and merciful in helping the babes in Christ. He performs miracles, even divine healing upon hearing the sincere cry of a new Christian endeavoring to seek Him and do His will. The Lord asks only that we knock and seek; through the Holy Spirit He does the rest.

The more we learn about divine healing and the effects of sin on the body, the more logical psychosomatic conditions become.

We cannot remain in willful sin and expect continuous blessings of divine healing. Sin causes anxiety, guilt, and other oppressing characteristics that upset the physiological nature of a person. Many of these can be explained by medical means.

Example of an illness that can be brought on by sin may be that of high blood pressure. This sort of an illness can well be caused by internal conflict, such as fears (disbelief in God), anxieties, and guilt feelings. These sins and oppressions can block divine healing. When a person cooperates with the grace that God gives and obeys the Holy Spirit, these sins can be overcome and healing can be obtained. Sometimes these are of an instantaneous nature—removal of the sin and removal of the physical affliction. This very often is evident in such cases as migraine headaches, narcotic addiction and alcoholism.

I have claimed healings and am still waiting for the complete victory over some of them. We can never understand everything as God understands it. But faith, positive confession and endurance are necessary qualities in a Christian and are essential if one is to receive divine healing.

An example of a man who went through many trials, due to error, was Job. Job failed in that he assumed self-righteousness and that God, therefore, was responsible for all his trials.

As his faith weakened, he left the door open for future affliction by the enemy.

Refer to the book of Job in times of tribulation, but keep
in mind certain considerations.

1. Be attentive to God's voice in matters of sanctification.
2. Recognize Satan as the bearer of all evil.
3. Humble yourself before God and His will.
4. Rebuke the enemy and his works.
5. Ask God to heal the affliction.

Seek God, pray, find the answers, do everything that God
wants done, then through faith (with a clear conscience),
receive evidence of the complete victory by positive, persistent
confession.

"My people are destroyed for lack of knowledge." [118]

Referring to the book of Job in time of stress and tribulation will enable you to see how heavy affliction was permitted
to be brought upon Job to strengthen and increase his devotion to God.

Miraculous healings are often done in a shorter span of
time than the body could naturally perform and in ways that
natural means cannot accomplish.

Instant healing in all cases would be catastrophic and
against the Word.

"If my people, which are called by my name,
shall humble themselves, and pray, and seek my face,
and turn from their wicked ways; then will I hear from heaven,
and will forgive their sin, and will heal their land." [119]

God deals with each individual through his spirit. If it is God's desire that something in a life be changed in order to receive a healing, some sin that must be relinquished, the person should ask God to remove the sin. That is exactly what He means to have done. Many have experienced this in alcoholism and its arrest.

Lack of spiritual education and spiritual yielding leads us into areas of ignorance. In times of illness one should seek God, pray, find the answers, and do everything that God wants done.

Be content to ask and receive as God gives, and proceed to search for more knowledge of Jesus Christ and greater victories. Certainly, not to ask is not to receive. To become more knowledgeable of Christ puts a Christian in a better position for greater spiritual achievements and greater glorification of God.

One must keep in mind that the abundant life is not the life of a whimpering, spoiled child of God, but rather the life of a spiritual athlete with the strength of the Holy Spirit.

"Know ye not that they which run in a race run all,
but one receiveth the prize? So run that ye may obtain." [120]

"The effectual fervent prayer of a righteous man availeth much." [121]

Shortly after receiving my bursitis healing, I was approached by a visiting evangelist. He wanted to know the name of a reputable pharmacist so that he could get a prescription filled. Having recently received my victory, I answered smugly, "I'm sorry, I can't help you there. I just don't need them anymore." To this he replied, "That's something we just don't understand. We minister divine healing and yet we still have afflictions come upon us."

Later, my recollection went back to the episode wherein I had been smug. At that time the Lord gave me II Corinthians 12:7. It was a time when Paul was afflicted with a thorn in the flesh, although the Scripture does not define whether Paul's thorn was a physical or spiritual one. I was impressed that a thorn in my side was my own smugness.

In this Scripture, we find that the purpose of Paul's thorn was to keep him humble. He asked the Lord to remove it, but he was informed:

"My grace is sufficient for thee: for my strength is made perfect in weakness. Most gladly therefore will I rather glory in my infirmities, that the power of Christ may rest upon me." [122]

The Lord has impressed upon me that healings are ministered because of the power of the Resurrection and the stripes of Jesus Christ, and one must not be puffed up as though this were a personal accomplishment.

Sometime ago, I prayed to the Lord that He remind me in advance of any self-seeking glory and let me know that I alone am nothing, and that all things come through Jesus Christ. I'm grateful that He continues to do so.

Since the above incident, I asked the Lord to forgive me for my smugness, and, unlike Paul, I have been freed to claim healing for my thorn. Everyone is subject to obedience to God's Word and can receive healings, when meeting God's conditions. This sometimes entails years of waiting, till God's purpose is fulfilled.

CANNIBALISM

Some people shy away from Christianity because of what they feel is the "cannibalistic" belief of consuming the Body and Blood of Christ, in Holy Communion.

The old and new covenants, as explained in the book of Hebrews, show how the priests of old continuously offered animals and used animal blood as the sacrifice for sin, until Christ's Body and Blood were sacrificed one time for all sins, for all men, for all time.

Communion is a small glass of grape juice and a wafer of unleavened bread. These are the symbols of the Body and Blood of Christ, of Christ's sacrifice at Calvary, for our sins and salvation. At the time of receiving Holy Communion, one should engage in personal introspection and repentance, and use this time to appreciate and reflect on Christ's great sacrifice. Communion is sharing in the remembrance of that occasion and should remind us of the devotion we should have to Christ and the dedicated lives we should live for His glory.

Christ, at the last supper, used the symbols of grape juice and bread. He spoke the words:

"This is my body which is given for you: this do in remembrance of me." [123]

"This cup is the new testament in my blood, which is shed for you." [124]

Neither Christ or His followers consumed blood. Christ's words represent His sacrifice and were to be a lasting memory of the "cup" He "drank" at Calvary.

*"...Father, if thou be willing, remove this cup from me,
nevertheless not my will, but thine, be done."* [125]

Scriptures warn against the consumption of blood:

*"But flesh with the life thereof, which is the blood thereof,
shall ye not eat."* [126]

*"But we write unto them, that they abstain from pollution of idols,
and from fornication, and from things strangled,
and from blood."* [127]

Cannibalism is a favorite trick of the enemy to discourage people from accepting Christ and the abundant life. This is because the Crucifixion backfired on the enemy and became the ultimate frustration that assured his eternal damnation.

Once a person accepts Christ as Saviour, the Lord, by His Holy Spirit, begins to grant revelations pertaining to the symbolism of Holy Communion.

EMOTIONALISM

People shy away from full-gospel Pentecostal worship and a deeper spiritual life because of their feelings toward emotionalism. This involves a fear categorized under pride.

None of us can show love without showing emotion. We know this to be true, because emotion exists in our personal lives through times of birth, death, illness and marriage, or in other seasons of life.

Circumstances, people, and families are real. In all these areas we show emotion. God is real, so why can't we show emotion toward Him? Is it because we are ashamed to show emotion toward God in front of other people as we are often ashamed to show emotion toward others?

Emotion should be shown more to God than to anyone else.

Flowing tears let me know that I am getting to the proper attitude in prayer. I begin to feel emotions toward God.

Now that I've worshipped with those who express emotion in the church assembly, I've had similar experiences in the assembly because I am not ashamed or afraid to show my emotions toward Him.

Victories are won at the foot of the cross in tearful repentance, in true humility. In a state of true humility, one prays till one reaches a point of admitting one's shortcomings and is able to put aside one's self-centeredness and pride. One submits to proper authority according to God's divine order and His Word. Honesty has been invoked and specific areas of disobedience have been recognized. A non-resisting will has been obligated, in a state of determination, to let God show other areas of rebellion in the future.

After praying thusly, one is in a state of ready obedience and trusts in God to work out all things. A total reliance exists in God to handle every situation. There is a peace that exceeds any other ever known. There is an acceptance of whatever God will permit to happen in the future. The evidence of this emerges in the fact that no matter what happens from day to day, we do not become disturbed. If we are disturbed, we need to go back to the cross and pray until once again we trust in God and resume living in the peace of that trust.

Missing the mark begins with a refusal to get on one's knees. A few praises, thanksgiving, and words acknowledging God's almightiness are not enough. These things bring joy, tears, and a relaxed feeling of righteousness and emotional release, but in themselves, they do not reflect true repentance and humility. The error shows itself in presuming that these feelings are justification from God, and we tend to believe that this puts us in good standing with God, that we are okay "as is." This state of good feelings is a deceptive state. Generally, without following up with prayer, one will continue to "suffer" under burdens, thinking of them as "persecutions." One assumes that he has done everything possible to draw close to God and be obedient to Him, but he sees little change in adverse circumstances. This is followed by a life in which the individual sees adversities only as God's testing of perseverance, in long-suffering. Self-righteousness reigns and the victory is missed while one continues to defend an erroneous position. The big door of improper emotionalism has closed the corridor of prayer completion and blinded the eyes of the person. This is another reason why one cannot go by one's feelings, whether in the assembly or in the prayer closet. All the following is then vain repetition, because the petitioner has not gotten through and cannot get through in that state.

This stage of emotionalism, I believe, is one of the gravest areas of Christian failure. There is continuous seeking of this state of emotional "well-being" and subsequent failure in the walk. This state of well-being can in no way compare with the real thing that follows completed prayer, and total reliance on God, instead of self. In the former, we try to control all things; in the latter, God has the reins, and changes come about, in us and in others.

Even the hardest person shows emotion on the death bed—whether it be through external signs such as hopeless weeping or by the internal signs of a pounding heart and increased blood pressure.

Emotion is a big part of life and consumes much energy. The use of this energy can result in bondage and a stifled existence, or growth.

In the A.A. program, most find that after they get onto the road to recovery, they can again show proper emotion; they can cry, they can laugh. It is discovered that emotions are part of a sane existence and that most energies had been wasted on the wrong emotions such as hate. On the road to sobriety, emotions can be put into proper balance.

This is the work of the Holy Spirit, that lives might eventually become filled with the Holy Spirit, thus producing the fruit of the Spirit.

WHY DO SOME THINGS HAPPEN?

Why do some things happen? This is a question in the minds of many, concerning God's mercy and goodness. We often reap what we sow and see the direct results in the life we live.

Generally speaking, things happen to turn people to Christ and salvation or to draw them to a closer walk and help them grow unto perfection. One will find certain hardships in life if he goes against the Word of God or lives in disbelief. Alcoholism turned me to Christ's power and salvation after I had tried for years to be a good boy and then to be a good man. Although I knew of Christ and felt that His judgment would have been in my favor, I was not aware that I had salvation; nor was there any power in my life.

We need to understand that God uses all things, according to His purpose, for our good. This is why all things do not go our way. It does not mean that we cannot make some things happen, but everyone finds frustration in attempting to do certain things. The frustration ends only when one submits to circumstances through God's Word. Life adventure and satisfaction are found in the net results.

"A man's heart deviseth his way,
but the Lord directeth his steps." [128]

"The lot is cast into the lap;
but the whole disposing thereof is of the Lord." [129]

People are sometimes stricken because they are rebellious toward God's will. After God has dealt with some for so long, and they continue in their rebellious ways, they are removed from the Earth. This might happen in an automobile accident, or a drinking spree, or some other similar situation.

"Let no man deceive you with vain words;
for because of these things cometh the wrath of God
upon the children of disobedience." [130]

We may have a grave resentment toward God because of the things the enemy brings into our lives. After I accepted Christ I discovered that, in my case, this was true. I had to repent of this and ask God to forgive me.

One must understand and accept that God cares for him and desires for all people:

1. to be saved through Jesus Christ,

2. to walk in Christ unto perfection through repentance.

Together these two comprise commitment unto perfection. Until these are accepted, there will be afflictions because of lack of armor of the Word.

In walking unto perfection, we are admonished to judge ourselves.

"For if we would judge ourselves, we should not be judged." [131]

If we judge ourselves honestly, God will not have to judge us, and we will be free from sin by the power of the Resurrection—by faith.

"But when we are judged, we are chastened of the Lord
that we not be condemned with the World." [132]

If God has to judge us, then we reap what we sow through affliction by the enemy, perhaps in the form of illness or severe strife. If we judge, confess and ask God to remove the sin, then we are in line with the Word and secure in that knowledge.

God deals in love, but the inborn sinful nature grows into self-love until one is blinded from seeing His love through Christ. This has been borne out to me while ministering to non-Christians, new babes in Christ, and many long-term Christians. The world is filled with people who are so deeply engrossed in themselves that they are in no position to give, share, or perform acts of love for anyone. Usually, after being a Christian for a while, one can extend Christ's love to others. Even then, there comes a time that the Christian has to look to Calvary and say, "Yes, Jesus, you did it for me and I will gladly follow." When that is done, the real joy of loving others becomes a reality. Then the Lord showers the servant with the true fruit of love, as well as other blessings, which often include material things desired.

We wonder, "Why?" when we hear about the death of a busload of school children or a large number of people on board an airplane. Children are not condemned for their actions under the age of accountability and are under God's protection until then. Adults and children beyond the age of accountability (the spiritual age is really known only to God) *are* responsible for their actions. God knows the condition, the heart and accountability of all; and the soul of each person is precious to our Lord, not the body alone.

Although the loss of a loved one may be very painful, regardless of how we view it, this experience is used by God in the best interests of everyone involved. These are the things that bring out our true attitude toward God.

Our attitude toward such things is formed around these situations:

1. Our lack of knowledge and judgment, which only God has in view of commitment unto perfection

2. Our relationship with God –

a. Non-Christian attitude

b. Christian attitude

A non-Christian attitude concludes with dissatisfaction, while the Christian attitude is one of spiritual renewal.

"And we know that all things work together for good to them that love God, to them who are the called according to His purpose." [133]

The human emotions still have to be dealt with, and grieving needs to take place for a season, but the truth of the Word must take precedence over self-pity and negativity.

GIVING UP THINGS AND BECOMING GOOD FIRST

People feel that in becoming a Christian, they will have to give up the so-called good things. They don't want to give up such things as drinking alcohol or smoking. To the human nature these things seem good until they are found to be serious hazards to mental, physical, and spiritual well-being. As opposed to the human nature, the spiritual nature continually seeks truly good things by absorbing God's Word and finding that God's way of living is the satisfying ultimate in the mental, physical, and spiritual realms.

Generally, most people will live for this world until God opens their ears during a time of oppression and brings them to the point of decision. This decision point is brought about by conviction of the Holy Spirit, an internal dissatisfaction— "Something is bothering me inside"—a slowly increasing anxiety in the later years about what will happen to them after death. Many people, unfortunately, are wiped out before they yield to the call. If you have been delaying making that decision, seriously consider making that decision now, so that you can have the abundant life.

One needs to decide if he will have the benefits of fellowship with God here on Earth and then live with Christ through eternity, or if he wants to live solely for this world and be eternally separated from God.

Naturally, when one accepts Christ, becomes a Christian, and seeks God, God will remove things from that person's life that he thought he might not want to part with. But God does so in such a way that one's personal life becomes enriched, as freedom from the flesh is progressively realized. The person then wants more of what God has to offer, along with the resulting positive changes.

The secret of success in making a decision for an abundant life is in first making the decision to accept Christ and the abundant life, by faith.

In facing a decision for Christ, some feel they need to become good first. One of the most beautiful parts of becoming a Christian is accepting Christ in the condition you are in and enjoying the adventure as He patiently rebuilds you.

If I had waited till I became good first, I would not have heeded the drawing of the Holy Spirit to repentance and would have died in the bottle. I discovered that I needed to find *God* first.

On my own merit and efforts I found that I could not give up alcohol, which was killing me and driving me to complete insanity. It is the grace of God that enabled me to see alcoholism arrested.

It is this same grace that enables us to see spiritual growth and the removal of sinful, self-damaging things from our lives. This is the freedom from bondage and part of the liberty in Christ. We know that we can't simply change our behavior. Behavior changes as a result of a change in our beliefs. Believing in God is "making a decision to turn our will and our life over to the care of God."

One's personal experience with Jesus is uniquely different from all others, with the assurance that one has eternal life in righteousness. One's heart in Christ and Christ in one's heart is the sanctuary of worship, growth, peace, joy and fellowship. The sanctuary becomes what we allow God to make it.

LIBERTY IN CHRIST

Liberty in Christ can dwell only in those committed to Christ, in obedience and faith toward God. It is a gift of God to His bondservants, made subject to His will, in His service. It is liberty from *sin, death, the devil,* and *the law.*

Service includes dedication to God, Christ, righteousness, and witnessing to others for furtherance of the gospel.

Liberty from sin occurs in the righteousness of the blood of Christ, shed at Calvary for all, who, by their own wills, accept Him as their Saviour. Only those under the blood are free from the penalties of sin. The Word is the Christian's guide; one's attitude toward it is reflected in his relationship with Jesus.

Liberty from death assures bodily resurrection for the Christian and eventual freedom from the temptations of sin, as won by Christ through His Resurrection.

Liberty from the devil is liberty from all the deceitful works of him and his kind. Grace is given by God for the defeat of backsliding, illness, temptation, unbelief, spiritual procrastination, and all other aspects of oppression and adversity. The battle is on! Satan pours on more effort and loses bigger every day, as the Christian defeats him by the grace of God and grows in the Spirit.

Liberty from law is confirmed in salvation through faith and not in works of the law, but rather in works of fruitfulness.

"Even so faith, if it hath not works, is dead, being alone.
Yea, a man may say, Thou hast faith, and I have works:

shew me thy faith without thy works,
and I will shew thee my faith by my works.
Thou believest that there is one God;
thou doest well: the devils also believe and tremble." [134]

The law has become the superstitious, ceremonial practices of the Old Testament, such as circumcision and observance of the Sabbath. Salvation includes subjection to God's will. Subjection to God's will includes the acceptance of the responsibilities of the law of liberty (His Word, under the new covenant of Christ) and is not free license. The Christian is subject to God's law as Christ taught it. The law of liberty means self-sacrifice for the good of souls and the glory of God. It is not freedom from any part of God's Word, but is a state of constant striving under grace, to obey the gospel. In this striving is surrender of self in following Christ, in the Spirit. It is not acceptance of a certain sin-level until God changes one. As in predestination, free will and spiritual perseverance in faith are factors in reaching for God's grace. Human wisdom (knowledge of the mind) in seeking righteousness and God's grace will not get one to heaven. Divine wisdom, walking in the Spirit of Christ, patience, hope, love, humility and complete trust in God are secrets of God's grace.

"For the Lord giveth wisdom:
out of his mouth cometh knowledge and understanding.
He layeth up sound wisdom for the righteous:
He is a buckler to them that walk uprightly." [135]

"For we through the Spirit wait for the hope of righteousness
by faith. For in Jesus Christ neither circumcision
availeth anything, nor uncircumcision;
but faith which worketh by love." [136]

"Trust in the Lord with all thine heart;
and lean not unto thine own understanding.
In all thy ways acknowledge him,
and He shall direct thy paths." [137]

Faith works through love—love of God, through God's first command; and love of man, per God's second command. Love of self is projected in one's sincere willingness to obey God's first and second commands.

Freedom is a state without any restraints. Liberty is partial freedom, as ordained by God, with restraints. License is a state, without restraints, granted to one person, but not to another.

"Verily I say unto you,
Whosoever shall not receive the kingdom of God
as a little child, he shall not enter therein." [138]

In this Scripture, Jesus was teaching about marriage and divorce, among other things. God equates one's coming to Christ as one contracting in marriage.

Today's computers are busily trying to match appropriate couples of mutual personalities, so that their marriages will succeed. God's plan is that two people come together for change. He uses people to help each other change and grow, by His Word, in place of their own and inherited erroneous convictions. The two are to become one, as God's children, subject to His divine order and His other spiritual laws.

So it is in becoming a Christian. One comes to Christ, to be subject to His Will, as a child of obedience. Everyone seeks fulfillment in some parental authority and security. This fulfillment comes through conformity to the Christ-like image, as seen in the boy Jesus. Christians are not robots nor are they fulfilled by logic or self-analysis. They are children of God, happy with their Parent (God, The Father), secure in His love and mercy.

REPENTANCE

Repentance means turning away from sins of commission and omission and turning to God. Love of God leads to contrition, which is the true meaning of spiritual repentance. Remorse is the guilt feeling resulting from sin, while attrition (imperfect contrition) is a mortal repentance arising from worldly motives, such as fear of punishment, the loss of friendship, or loss of sobriety. Spiritual repentance involves regret over the sin and resolve to change one's mind regarding its occurrence. It is accomplished with the purpose of making amends.

As the Holy Spirit discerns the thoughts and intents of the heart, God intends for certain steps to be taken:

1. Admission of sin to self, another person, and God

2. A change in attitude

3. Amendment – a change for the better and righting the wrong done.

4. Continued obedience to the Holy Spirit in place of the previous rebellion and resistance, until God completely removes the sin

An additional action that is a greater step of faith and a faith-builder is to attain the place where one can admit the past bondage to anyone, declaring that Jesus is the victor and the ongoing keeper of victory. Until one dares take this action, he cannot spiritually understand it or receive the resulting blessings.

Judas betrayed Jesus and hung himself in *remorse,* on the way to hell.

Man's will and repentance are of the utmost importance in reaching out for the grace of God.

One of the revelations the Lord gave me as I wrote this book is the increasing significance of the command of "obedience and faith," which was given to me in the vision of "Sodom and Gomorrah." It can be interpreted as repentance and trust (faith) in Him. Salvation is contingent on the integration of obedience and faith in the Christian's life. First and last in His ministry, Jesus commanded obedience and faith in Him.

> *"...Thus it is written, and thus it behooved Christ to suffer,*
> *and to rise from the dead the third day:*
> *and that repentance and*
> *remission of sins should be preached*
> *in his name among all nations, beginning at Jerusalem.*
> *And ye are witnesses of these things."* [139]

Love for God brings repentance, which fulfills His command of love for Him and one's fellowman. Lack of remorse and true repentance results from hardening of the heart and brings fruitlessness. This constitutes a life with trust in self instead of trust in God and leaves the door of affliction open to the enemy.

Honestly taking all the Steps in A.A., I was freed from the bondage of alcoholism. Some have continued to grow by continuing in the Steps. Others have found Christ and are growing in the Word. Still others are continuing in the Steps and are searching, knowing that there is more.

Some failed in A.A. because of dishonesty and indulgence in remorse or attrition in place of true repentance.

"For Godly sorrow worketh repentance to salvation
not to be repented of:
but the sorrow of the world worketh death." [140]

Those of us in A.A. balked at attending churches or listening to church people because they did not understand our way of life, our program. They basically do not understand the full-time spiritual earnestness required in overcoming the bondage of alcoholism, or that sometimes one needs to put on a pot of coffee and sit up all night to talk about God and share his "guts." This situation remains pretty much the same today. We kept sober by confessing one to another, sharing our common denominator—alcoholism—while encouraging each other.

The kingdom of God is implanted and nourished in the hearts of men, which make up the true Church. The Church is not religion or denominations or buildings.

"God that made the world and all things therein,
seeing that He is Lord of heaven and earth,
dwelleth not in temples made with hands." [141]

God desires a repentant blessed people as part of His eternal plan. Love, repentance, faith, and spiritual growth go hand in hand. Those who put these elements into practice, by the grace of God, will move out and see God's power in fruitfulness. They will spread the gospel that others may know of salvation and become part of the Church body, as born-again disciples.

Sober alcoholics are thankful for their sobriety and the spiritual growth gained through their Twelve Step program of repentance. We have much to share in what God has done for us.

Repentance is one of the most difficult things for people to achieve, but is most vital to progress. It is imperative that a person repent daily.

"But exhort one another daily, while it is called today;
lest any of you be hardened through the deceitfulness of sin." [142]

God responds to repentance.

"If my people, which are called by my name,
shall humble themselves,
and pray and seek my face, and turn from their wicked ways;
then will I hear from heaven, and will forgive their sin,
and will heal their land." [143]

Different degrees of submission bring different degrees of growth. Partial repentance brings partial results.

"Be ye therefore perfect,
even as your Father which is in heaven is perfect." [144]
"Not as though I had already attained,
either were already perfect:

but I follow after, if that I may apprehend that for which also I am apprehended of Christ Jesus." [145]

In A.A., we looked at the Steps for the first time and each of us said, "I can't go through with it." If we practiced partial discipline and partial repentance, we practiced self-dishonesty and this resulted in self-deception. We had to strive for as complete a repentance as possible and daily repentance thereafter.

The Lord will draw the boundaries as to what extent a person goes to at a particular time. He seems to establish larger boundaries if the effort is greater. One loses spiritual benefits when one establishes those boundaries himself through spiritual laziness, pride and fear.

There usually is little response to the call of repentance through God's love of promised blessings, while a person is all-willing on the deathbed. Alcoholics are put at the foot of the cross because progress is necessary for survival. It is not a luxury. Most alcoholics have long since passed the love approach. The Lord permits us to have our way, living under control of the enemy, until we bow before Him. Unfortunately most people do not heed His loving call to promised blessings until they become desperate for His help.

"For we are consumed by thine anger, and by thy wrath we are troubled." [146]

We reap what we ourselves have sown until we are brought to our knees.

God accepts anyone who will come, but He requires repentance for salvation. With repentance, we grow spiritually. With Christ, we grow spiritually and have inner witness of eternal life with Him.

Striving to heed the Lord's call to repentance has brought major victories in my Christian walk. I am grateful that God has shown me the value in gut-level communication and the reality of His promise to heal spiritually through true repentance and reliance on Him.

The A.A. way of creating a self-inventory, written over a period of months, followed by the making of amends to others, is rarely heard of outside A.A. and other twelve-step groups. This method of repentance preparation has been a major asset toward my achieving the liberties in Christ. However, it is gratifying to see beautiful Christians who have learned the true value of repentance, through the guidance of the Holy Spirit.

A practical method of repentance, such as the Twelve Steps of A.A., is also generally unknown, taught or applied. Where I have seen attempts to use the Steps, it has been done on "schedule" and/or without contrition. The execution I saw was mechanical because of pride, fear, and a lack of belief that God can change people. The results were largely fruitless. Initial repentance takes as long as is required to get spiritual confirmation that it is complete. In most cases I think that would involve at least a year of prayer, inventory, and making amendments.

We know the difficulty in facing our own self-image and subjecting it to change, in opposition to the ego's demands.

Responsible, confrontational (gut-level) communication is very strenuous at best, and often requires going off to brood for a while before coming back for more. Returning to deal with the little boy or girl inside and admitting our wrongs to our gut-level communicator has proven to be an asset toward permanent release from bondage.

Sometimes it is necessary to back away from a potential communicator because of a lack of ability to face the truth about ourselves and respond in a constructive manner. It is overwhelming to find the number of people in bondage, pastors included, due to immaturity in this area. Spiritual bondage becomes readily discernible, as one grows in the Word, after having executed true initial repentance. I feel that this is one of the key areas in which God will move to bring the Church into proper perspective, as part of the bride of Christ. This is my observation and evaluation of God's Word.

Repentance has been the key issue of salvation since John and Jesus commanded it. I believe most people feel that the act of accepting Christ as Saviour is initial repentance. The act gives one eternal life with God and is a part of repentance in that it is an agreement to give up the rebellious attitude of running one's own life and pledging to allow God to take control. After that, the righteousness in Christ is claimed and an initial concentrated, past-life, soul-search is seldom thought of. In such a state, one continues in proud family traditions (passed-down sins of the fathers), which keep one in insecurities and other bonds, contrary to the Word of God.

I appreciate the few who have been gut-level communicators in fellowship with me and the fact that I have much to learn in the mechanics of this true spiritual fellowship.

Although God works in many ways, I feel that we need not fear that gut-level communication will become a corrupting custom in the world or in the Church.

An atmosphere of security does not generally exist in the Church as it does in A.A., where all admit to a common affliction and work together with compassion and without cliques for the sole purpose of mutual growth. There is an atmosphere of fear of confession that others will see the sin, often a false air of sinlessness and, a hopelessness for anyone seeking that secure atmosphere in the churches, after an A.A. spiritual experience.

I feel that when God says "repent" to one who has accepted Christ, He is not saying, "You better shape up, buddy, or I'm gonna hit you with a ball of fire and brimstone." I believe He is saying, "I have given you *physical* life, you have accepted *eternal* life, now let me give you *spiritual* life."

There are so many aspects of every life that are affected by repentance, or the lack of, that it would take volumes to cover the subject.

Appropriating From God

The ability to appropriate from God, or to have prayers answered, is important to everyone. The following comments on prayer and appropriating from God are intended to help those who need help in the prayer area. The important thing to remember is that we should talk to God from our heart. There are times when we receive answers from just plain talking to Him, with a sincere heart, in simple language. We should not be preoccupied with ritual or prayer outlines, but rather, with our own sincerity and God's will for our lives.

Again, obedience and faith are the keys to appropriating from God. We have previously covered the need for grace, which is the only way anything can be accomplished.

All prerequisites for appropriation are set forth in the "Lord's Prayer," the perfect prayer taught by Jesus.

Although the prayer has been named "The Lord's Prayer," it is really our prayer. Christ was perfectly obedient to the Father and was sinless. Therefore He could never say this prayer as we do.

"After this manner therefore pray ye." [147]

Consciously accepting Christ and acknowledging Him as our Saviour brings further meaning in meditation upon "our Prayer."

In the book of Matthew, "our Prayer" is preceded by another instruction, which becomes even more meaningful through divine wisdom and revelation.

"For the Lord giveth wisdom: out of his mouth cometh
knowledge and understanding." [148]

Jesus taught that prayer should not be prolonged in front of men, so as to be hypocritical. He directed secret (secluded) prayer that He might reward openly.

"And when thou prayest, thou shalt not be as the hypocrites
are: for they love to pray standing in the synagogues and in the
corners of the streets, that they may be seen of men.
Verily I say unto you, they have their reward.
But thou, when thou prayest, enter into thy closet,
and when thou hast shut the door, pray to thy Father
which is in secret; and thy Father which seeth in secret
shall reward thee openly." [149]

He also instructed us not to pray in vain repetition.

"But when ye pray, use not vain repetitions as the heathen do:
for they think that they shall be heard for their much speaking.
Be not ye therefore like unto them: for your Father knoweth
what things ye have need of, before ye ask him." [150]

Understanding by God's grace, will reveal several points in regard to the above Scriptures:

1. A Christian's prayers are heard by God through evidence of obedience and faith.

2. God responds to the Christian's prayers that are said in obedience and faith.

3. God knows everyone's needs "before ye ask."

4. Faith is the bridge between accepting God's answer and seeing the work completed.

5. God answers prayers according to His will.

6. Fruitfulness comes through surrender of the "old man" and the flesh (self).

7. The walk in the Spirit is walking with God, not working for Him.

8. Love is not selfish.

To summarize the above: Any person crying out to God, searching for Christ, and especially a new Christian, often prays the best way he knows: repetitiously and selfishly. God honors these sincere prayers because knowledge of His Word and understanding by His divine wisdom are not yet instilled in the petitioner, and whose basic need is for self.

In the past, I often prayed memorized prayers, repetitiously, during which time my mind would often wander to things far from God, to no avail.

After initial energies are spent on self and attaining a certain position of growth in the Word, the Christian begins to face the death of the old man and learns that one of the secrets of growth, answered prayer, and fruitfulness is turning from the needs of self and turning to the needs of others. Only God can reveal this, at the right time and under the conditions of His will. God will give the assurance of personal needs being met, with growing trust in Him. Repetitious "asking" in prayer diminishes as faith grows, and the repetition instead becomes thankfulness for the victory. Repetitious asking occurs with less frequency as it is transformed into asking God to do a work in a particular area toward the victory.

We go on to bear the fruit of long-suffering and to develop an honesty concerning our personal spiritual poverty. God gives conviction of victory in the petitioner's trust (faith) and turns the energies (prayers) toward other's needs, with spiritual satisfaction. This is followed by fruitfulness, as confirmation of God's grace.

Along with this comes the realization that grace comes through moving with God and giving self for others, as Christ gave Himself for us. It does not come by exhaustively working for God in every busy activity of the Church. One who places himself in God's work will not have spiritual witness of that position. Prayer, obedience, and faith will move one into God's work and God's will. Each one must pray according to the knowledge and the grace given.

Our Prayer

"Our Father which art in heaven, Hallowed be thy name.
Thy kingdom come. Thy will be done in earth, as it is in heaven.
Give us this day our daily bread. And forgive us our debts,
as we forgive our debtors. And lead us not into temptation,
but deliver us from evil: For thine is the kingdom, and the power,
and the glory, forever, Amen." [151]

"Our Prayer" covers all necessary facets of daily petition for meeting the physical and spiritual needs:

Glorification of God
Acknowledgment of

    His love

    God as the administrator of grace

    God as the divine ruler—His laws, His word

    God's sovereignty

    Liberty In Christ, through the Holy Spirit

    Required obedience—now and after Christ's second coming

Meeting the Petitioner's Needs
Petition for

    Grace to do God's will

    Material needs

    Laborers and willingness to be a laborer

    Grace to confess sins and make amends

    The fruit of the Spirit

    Forgiveness through Christ

    Grace to forgive others

    Shelter from temptation

    Grace for growth through trials and afflictions

    Eventual end of all evil

Let's go to church or to the prayer closet for a minute, assuming we have approached the throne, through "our Prayer."

"Behold, I stand at the door and knock:

if any man hear my voice,

and open the door, I will come in to him,

and I will sup with him,

and he with me." [152]

Keeping in mind all those things we have outlined above as our desire, acknowledgment, and willingness to do and let God do in our lives, we sit at the table He has prepared for us. He has set before each one a covered plate for our growth and His glory. On the plate is His Word, specifically chosen for each to be taken under direction of the Holy Spirit. After we uncover the plate, do we pick and choose? Do we take part of what He has served and turn our noses up at the rest? Do we push the plate aside unfinished and turn to our neighbor and indulge in things of the world, in preference? Is He anguished at our lack of interest in His nourishment?

He wants us to be strong and faithful. Have we pushed away His love for us? The "spinach" of repentance must be taken with the "dessert" of His joyful blessings, or we don't have the whole meal. This is what He meant when He invited us to eat and drink freely. This is what He meant when He said "If you love me, you will keep my commandments." If we don't eat and drink freely as God serves, we are not accepting the cup, as Christ accepted the cup at Gethsemane, and the living waters cannot flow through us to others. We have not supped with Him. We know what we have left on the plate, and our heart knows we have not eaten. Each subsequent return to the table finds the same portion, until we become undernourished, unfruitful, self-indulgent and complacent. What a joy it should be to eagerly look to the next meal with Him, in prayer, in the Word, to see what He will serve today. We should not be content with only dessert, unless we are content to remain a babe and live in immaturity. All dessert makes a cream-puff Christian, a good balanced diet makes a good soldier, ready for spiritual battle.

In becoming "as a child," we must realize it is in becoming obedient to the authority of God—in accepting His bread, His will, His Word as His voice, His love, His grace. We don't "earn" anything, but we are required to do our duty.

"So likewise ye, when ye shall have done all those things which are commanded you, say, We are unprofitable servants: we have done that which was our duty to do." [153]

Scripture and further comments on items of prayer are listed below, followed by a recommended prayer outline, which may be amended to fit the individual needs.

Love the Lord – Minister Unto Him

We are so accustomed to approaching God only when we want a favor, or perhaps when we are in dire need, that we fail to consider that a part of love is to give as well as receive.

"Thou are worthy, O Lord,
to receive glory and honour and power:
For thou hast created all things,
and for thy pleasure they are
and were created." [154]

God does not need us as we need Him. But we were created for fellowship with God, just as Adam and Eve were. When we consider the many things the Lord has done for us through Jesus Christ, we have much to be thankful for and we have a lot to love Him for, and we have numerous reasons to minister unto Him.

Acknowledge His Almightiness

"I know that thou canst do everything, and that no thought
can be withholden from thee." [155]

It is not only pleasing to God for us to acknowledge His almightiness, but it serves to remind us that without God, and without the intercession of Jesus Christ, we have nothing and we are nothing.

"O wretched man that I am! Who shall deliver me from the body
of this death? I thank God through Jesus Christ, Our Lord." [156]

Thanksgiving

Closely associated with ministering to God and acknowledging His almightiness is Thanksgiving. The more we grow in Jesus Christ, the more we have to be thankful to God for.

"Offer unto God thanksgiving; and pay thy vows unto the most High." [157]

"Be careful for nothing; but in everything by prayer and supplication with thanksgiving let your requests be made known unto God." [158]

Pray According to God's Will

"And this is the confidence that we have in him, that, if we ask anything according to his will, he heareth us. And if we know that he hear us, whatsoever we ask, we know that we have the petitions that we desired of him." [159]

Pray with Forgiveness and Confession

"Confess your faults one to another, and pray one for another that ye may be healed. The effectual fervent prayer of a righteous man availeth much." [160]

"For if ye forgive men their trespasses, your heavenly Father

will also forgive you: But if ye forgive not men their trespasses,
neither will your Father forgive your trespasses." [161]

Pray with Contrition

"If my people, which are called by my name,
shall humble themselves,
and pray, and seek my face, and turn from their wicked ways,
then will I hear from heaven, and will forgive their sin
and will heal their land." [162]

Pray with Love

Keep God's commandments.

"Herein is love, not that we loved God, but that he loved us,
and sent his Son to be the propitiation for our sins.
Beloved, if God so loved us, we ought also to love one another.
No man has seen God at any time. If we love one another,
God dwelleth in us, and his love is perfected in us." [163]

"And whatsoever we ask, we receive of him,
because we keep his commandments,
and do those things that are pleasing in his sight.
And this is his commandment,

That we should believe on the name
of his Son Jesus Christ, and love one another,
as he gave us commandment." [164]

"If ye abide in me, and my words abide in you, ye shall ask
what ye will, and it shall be done unto you." [165]

Pray with Purity

"Ye ask and receive not, because ye ask amiss, that ye may
consume it upon your lusts." [166]

Pray with Faith

"Therefore I say unto you, what things soever ye desire,
when ye pray, believe that ye receive them,
and ye shall have them." [167]

The above Scriptures and comments are important in appropriating from God. Some of these help to set the proper relationship with God, in fellowship, while other distinct conditions noted, are commanded for appropriating from God.

Lack of understanding can be overcome by seeking God. It is ignorance of Scriptural prayer instruction, deliberate disobedience, or rebellion that will keep a person from appropriating from God, or from experiencing much spiritual growth. The only one who truly knows if these conditions are met is the praying person. A person's heart, in the sight of God, is what will determine largely whether a prayer is heard and answered.

For any circumstance, God's will is clearly defined in the Word. Through prayer and seeking God, His will can become known.

One cannot meet these conditions by merely reading them. It takes time, prayer, understanding, and grace.

Prayer outline

Ministry to God and petitions of fellowship with Him:

Almightiness	Contrition
Thanksgiving	Love
God's Will	Purity Motive
Confession	Faith
Forgiveness	

"Listening" to God.

Petitions for others, self and other causes:

Praying for:

Spouse

Children

Salvation for friends (and enemies)

New converts

The Church

Conclusion may be final thanksgiving to God for hearing your prayers and giving the victory for all things included in your petitions (fruit of the Spirit, grace unto perfection, gifts, etc.)

"I beseech You therefore, brethren, by the mercies of God,

that ye present your bodies a living sacrifice, holy,

acceptable unto God, which is your reasonable service.

And be not conformed to this world: but be ye transformed

by the renewing of your mind,

that ye may prove what is that good,

and acceptable, and perfect will of God." [168]

These are Scriptures of sanctification which state the results obtainable by reaching for and obtaining grace. This should clearly make it understandable to any person that without the knowledge of the Word of God, and the understanding of God's will, how little can be accomplished.

Through the power of the Resurrection, we are sanctified. The Scriptures of sanctification will help determine one's "batting average" of gratitude and obedience toward God.

Although one should be open to repentance (if God speaks in such terms to one's heart when praying to Him), all things can be appropriated from God only because of the Atonement, through prayer with a sincere heart, and by recognizing Christ as Intercessor and Redeemer.

Having done the best we can to do God's will, we walk with a clear conscience. The only reason we can kneel before

God in prayer and be heard is that Jesus Christ died for all our sins, that we be made worthy to boldly approach God. It is His blood shed for our sins that is the Atonement. When we stand before God in prayer, having done our best, we stand in His eyes,—uncondemned, in the name of Jesus Christ.

Because of Christ's intercession and the power of the Resurrection, the Lord continues to bless us with freedom from bondage, despite our weaknesses, as long as we fight the battle with a pure heart. Gifts and callings are without repentance of God and are freely given by God, therefore one should be careful not to judge spiritual love and growth merely by gifts and blessings received.

God calls us to accept Christ. He calls us to the Word. He requires repentance and growth. He requires commitment unto perfection. Spiritual "status quo" results from rejecting the call for the next step of growth.

What also helps in our establishing a fellowship with God and improving our conscious relationship with Him are singing and humming spiritual songs of worship and praise, listening to spiritual recordings, fasting.

I lived the experience that let me know that God means business. I was totally helpless when God lifted me up. As it is said in the A.A. Program, "By the Grace of God."

It's one thing to say, "I know," but another to have been there! After sobriety came, I could then see lives transformed through tragedy—perhaps a family death, a severe auto accident, or other mishap. It became evident to me that God uses these things to draw us to Him. Praise God that He is always willing and waiting for us to come to the foot of the cross, or some of us would never make it.

I have experienced the sweetness of confessing to another, and also the broken bondage of sin and I have learned that the result was burnt bridges that I can never cross again, nor want to. These are some of the things that give me reason to be grateful for my conversion through alcoholism.

FRUIT OF THE SPIRIT

The fruit of the spirit is the yardstick by which everything in our lives is measured. The fruit is made up of grace-given qualities, opposed to the works of the flesh.

"For the fruit of the Spirit is in all goodness
and righteousness and truth." [169]

The Christian strives to replace works of the flesh with fruit of the Spirit.

The Fruit

"But the fruit of the Spirit is love, joy, peace,
longsuffering, gentleness,
goodness, faith, meekness, temperance:
against such there is no law." [170]

Love – God's goodness and mercy toward us; our adoration and devotion toward God; and charitable, self-sacrifice for others

Joy – extreme happiness resulting from good

Peace – freedom from mental and physical afflictions

Long-suffering – long-term patience

Gentleness – friendly in nature; of a kind disposition

Goodness – morally perfect, honorable, righteous, virtuous

Faith – belief in God, His sovereignty, His works

Meekness – having a patient, submissive, compliant nature

Temperance – constant moderation

Works of the Flesh

"Now the works of the flesh are manifest,
which are these; Adultery, fornication, uncleanness,
lasciviousness, idolatry, witchcraft, hatred,
variance, emulations, wrath, strife, seditions, heresies, envyings,
murders, drunkenness, revelings, and such like: of the which
I tell you before, as I have also told you in time past, that they
which do such things shall not inherit the kingdom of God." [171]

Adultery – participation in sex by a married person with other than spouse

Fornication – participation in sex by an unmarried person with others; word often used in Scriptures to point out other spiritual impurities, as well as adultery

Uncleanness – partaking in forms of sexual perversion

Lasciviousness – lustfulness, sensuality, that which produces lewd emotions and leads to uncleanness

Idolatry – idol worship

Witchcraft – practice of power of evil spirits, sorcery, fortune telling

Hatred – extreme dislike or animosity, general resentment

Variance – erroneous differing, dissension, discord

Emulations – ambition to equal or excel another in selfish rivalry

Wrath – violent anger, furious indignation, vengeance

Strife – angry contention, contest for selfish superiority or advantage

Seditions – language or conduct against peace and order, incitement of dissension or rebellion against authority

Heresies – any belief or opinion that is contrary to God's Word

Envying – resentment or discontentment over another's achievements or possessions

Murders – malicious killing of a human being in thought or deed, suicide

Drunkenness – inebriation by alcohol or other powerful stimulant, narcotic addiction

Revelings – to take delight in carousing or over-indulgence

In the beginning, as Christians, we study the Scripture about the fruit of the Spirit and see the things that we must have in our lives to be fruitful. Fruitfulness is having the fruit exemplified in us and through our works of faith. This results in spreading the gospel, helping others to come to Christ that they also might grow in the fruit. Self-discipline is required in appropriating and practicing fruitfulness and the fruit. There is a constant endeavor to achieve the fruit within one's self. We reach a point in the kingdom where we have righteousness in Christ, peace, and a joy, as administered by the Holy Spirit.

Nothing is possible except through the Resurrection, and the power therein. We claim our righteousness through that power, and subsequently, the fruit begins to show in our lives.

At this point, we have just touched on the kindergarten in the school of the fruit of the Spirit, and need to guard against self-satisfaction. We have attained fruit but need to go on to the spiritual level of fruitfulness. We are still much in the soul part of our three elements and all wrapped up in the "self" (selfish) part.

The main element that many lack, and prohibits one from going on to higher degrees of fruitfulness, is perfect love. A true love for God, for fellow man, and for one's self. The way to achieve a true love for God is through His Word, looking beyond self-satisfaction.

Love of self is self-acceptance resulting from recognition of weaknesses, righteousness only through Jesus Christ, a clear conscience in obedience to the Holy Spirit, and honesty in striving to do God's will under His law of love.

God's love creates a compassion deep within us to the point that we are sometimes anguished in our concern for others. To have that love, to exercise it, requires nonresistance to God and His word, and a willingness to grow, to go beyond "self," and to be shown by the Spirit of God and by others that He uses in our lives to show us our defects.

Growing in God's love also is accomplished through submission, one to another as per the Scripture. As we go on in this particular phase, we have to love by faith, also through the power of the Resurrection. We ask God to give us love in our hearts, which He does.

This love grows to a point where it helps us to throw our hands up to the Lord, asking Him to fill us with love, compassion for souls, and helps us to step out and witness to others, and see them come to the saving knowledge of Jesus Christ, to see them brought beneath the blood of Jesus and the power of the Resurrection. This means to see their souls saved: to see them come to salvation and the abundant life, where they can first begin to see the fruit of the Spirit in their own lives and go on in the ministry of reconciliation, and to see fruit in other's lives.

This is the place where we begin to become discontented with self-satisfaction—with accepting God's blessings and keeping them to ourselves, and with looking for more for ourselves. We should want everything that God has for us. But if we don't advance beyond this stage, then we are as smiling clanging cymbals!

To move on to a true spiritual life, we must see the bearing of fruit not just in ourselves. We also must extend this idea to others. We must see the fruit in everything we participate in. We must see it in our ministries, our homes. If we don't have fruit extending to others, or showing in what we participate in our station of life, we are not extending the love of Jesus Christ.

We must learn to look beyond ourselves in judging by the fruit of the Spirit, for it is not fruit of the body, fruit of the soul, or the fruit of "self." It is truly fruit of the Holy Spirit of God.

Nothing can give the kind of joy, peace, and satisfaction as the tear-stained, smiling face of a person who has just accepted Jesus Christ. The love that you have asked for, prayed for in faith, which the Lord has given you, at that moment shows in the face of those you have witnessed to—those you have helped to bring to the saving knowledge of Jesus Christ.

This all goes back to the cry for the Church that the Lord wants, free of spots and wrinkles, for the coming of Christ.

In keeping God's commandments we must learn to rise above self, get into His Word and face it for what it is. We must be able to learn from the faithful ones, whom the Lord puts into our lives to show us how selfish and proud we are. We must learn to hear these words, read them and recognize the Fruit and all the Word as our measuring yardstick. We must be able to be hurt within self and must be able to yield to God and recognize the fact that we are nothing without His grace, that we are so much "self." We need to be able to accept hurt, so that we can turn to God more sincerely and truly say, "Lord, yes, I am concerned with self. Grant me grace and a passion for souls. Help me to love others by faith. Help me to love your Word, that I may grow in it and adhere to it. Help me to go beyond myself so that my life may be truly spiritual."

If we cannot be hurt and then come back to love God, love His Word, and love those that may injure us in trying to be truthful in the Spirit, we cannot grow. We must be willing to let God change us so that we may be fruitful in all things.

When we yield to God and overcome the initial ill feelings that may arise, then we can feel a true joy and a true peace and a true compassion for souls. We have a satisfaction that we could not have until we go beyond self. If we come back, confessing our sins one to another, acknowledging self, and self-righteousness, then the Lord gives us grace to strive to obey Him and His Word, to show true spiritual fruitfulness in bringing others to Christ and living in the station wherein we are called, in a spiritual sense.

The results of accepting this challenge, which has been conquered by the power of the Resurrection, bring the true fruit of the Spirit, the tear-stained, smiling faces to the alter to accept Jesus. It opens the Word to them that they might follow in the ministry of reconciliation, which Jesus Himself gave to the apostles and to every Christian.

Accepting the challenge and conquering it, true fruitfulness will spring out of our lives from every aspect. Then we don't have to worry about self, because the fruit is there also. It cannot help but be there because we have stepped beyond ourselves to a true spiritual walk with the Lord, Jesus Christ.

A most important factor in obtaining genuine fruit is the motive behind the work. Works for self-glorification result in artificial fruit. Genuine fruit glorifies God and is all-pleasing in His eyes.

Previously we discussed the ability to discern which communication comes from God and which comes from the enemy. Honestly investigating the motive, verifying it with several Scriptures (primarily the law of love) and testing it by application of the fruit and the resulting fruitfulness will let us know the path to take.

> *"Even so every good tree bringeth forth good fruit;*
> *but a corrupt tree bringeth forth evil fruit."* [172]

The enemy is very deceptive and does all he can to make one believe that a wrong thought or action will bring good fruit. The result is always a work of the flesh. Sometimes one will need to wait for further communication to verify the goodness value of a contemplated action, rather than to act in haste. When any doubt or "internal voice" presents caution, one should not act at all. Eventually proper confirmation will come, through waiting on the Lord. Thought and action is discernible by the spirit, not the soul (feelings).

As a drunk, I chose my level of "bottom" on the elevator of alcoholism, by the grace of God. I trust God to take me all the way, on the elevator of His grace, to perfection in my quest for the fruit of the Spirit. This is the fulfillment of what I have waited for in gaining sobriety—receiving love from God and then sharing it with others. It is my reason for being alive and it is the answer to, "What's life all about?"

COMMITMENT UNTO PERFECTION

Commitment unto perfection concerns the fellowship between God and mankind and the work done in mankind through God's grace. Spiritual perfection means moving with God in a "clear conscience of heart," with resulting fruit of the Spirit. Fruit can show outwardly but fruitlessly with an imperfect heart.

Perfection, while on Earth, is very difficult because of ever-existing temptation.

The eventual glorified perfection and sinlessness will exist in an atmosphere without temptation.

Perfection means to become Christ-like, to live according to the law of love.

Obedience, faith, love, repentance, charity, self-control, and patience are the key factors in maintaining perfection in God's grace. Glorified perfection, in Christ, will be God's gift to Christians at the first resurrection, the Second Coming of Christ.

Frustration results from presuming, moving ahead of, or lagging behind God's grace. Grace here concerns being an overcomer and differs from the saving grace of salvation. Overcoming grace is given by God for growth toward perfection. Without initial repentance at the time of accepting Christ, it is highly unlikely that a person will understand the availability of overcoming grace.

Only God has always been, is, and always shall be all perfect. Christ was made perfect by suffering the price of obedience through temptation to fulfill His God-ordained ministry. His perfection was different from ours in that He was perfectly obedient to the Father, and had no need for substantiation as a man.

Our perfection is formed in being an overcomer. As we carry our cross of trials and afflictions, we walk toward Calvary to resurrection and glorification.

Three points are necessary to know in one's commitment:

1. Perfection is not measured by law-keeping.

2. Perfection is not sinlessness, but involves striving for total sinlessness.

3. Maturity in the fruit of the Spirit is the goal of one's commitment unto perfection.

In striving for sinlessness, one has to deal with sins of omission and sins of commission.

Sins of omission result from not doing good things that we know to do. These exist if we accept the fallacious idea that if we don't do anything bad, we are not sinning.

"Therefore to him that knoweth to do good,
and doeth it not, to him it is sin." [173]

Examples of sins of omission include the following –

Refusal to:
Read the Bible regularly

Act on the Scriptural knowledge we have

Let self die – be broken

Counteract gossip and untruths

Assemble with other Christians

Pray

Witness of Christ

Tithe

Accept family responsibilities

Help orphans, widows, elders and those who are handicapped

Vote

Weigh motive before acting

Confess sins and repent of them

Examples of sins of commission contain these:

Pride

Lying

All works of the flesh

Neglect of repenting of sins of omission and commission hinders the realization of consecration or walking in the Spirit. Yielding or nonresistance to the Holy Spirit brings the abundant life.

One might think that carrying a cross to Calvary is some abundant life! I have dragged the cross behind me in rebellion and now I have Jesus in my heart and the cross on my shoulder. I find it gratifying and easier, with the help of Christ, than the old way with total self on the throne.

Accepting repentance has brought liberty in Christ, with all the blessings of God. Honest initial repentance brought freedom from alcoholism and grace to accept Jesus Christ and forgiveness of my past sins. The grace of God is bringing the fruits and fruitfulness into my life.

"O fear the Lord, ye his saints: for there is no want
to them that fear him.
...but they that seek the Lord shall not want any good thing." [174]

Confession of sins brings forgiveness of sins, and is a part of repentance, per the word of God. Confession to self is admission of sin. There remains the confession to God and to man. All sins are against God and must be confessed to Him. Some sins are against God and man. Those committed against God and man must be dealt with by making confession to God and amendment to the person one has sinned against. Overcoming grace covers only those sins repented of, as the Holy Spirit convicts.

There is a resistance to confession to man because of the pain of humility involved. Without that humility, though, one never realizes the healing benefits and instead remains in bondage.

"Whosoever therefore shall humble himself as this little child,
the same is greatest in the Kingdom of heaven." [175]

After confession to man, it is easier to confess to God. Without exercising humility in confession to man, one can hardly admit the sin to God, without further conviction, knowing only God can forgive the sin.

Another reason for resistance to confession to man is the fear of ridicule and condemnation. In place of ridicule and condemnation, practice of love and praying for one another, encourages confession and benefits all in strength and healing. Condemnation by man is nothing, when the condemnation of God is considered!

I am happy to say that each confession I made to anyone, and each time I asked for forgiveness, while taking the Twelve Steps, was received in the right spirit. Each person accepted the amendment, to the best of my knowledge, and I was relieved from any associated burden. Those approached by letter, or some other means of communication, who did not respond at all may carry the burden of an unforgiving spirit and guilt of their own sins.

In A.A., we recognized each other as repentant sinners and experienced the freedom from pride that had hindered us from confessing. We confessed to each other not only sins against man but many of those things that only God knew about. Some openly confessed from the speaker's podium, telling their story, exhibiting honesty and a strong foundation of sobriety, according to the grace given. We sat with tear-filled eyes, in compassion for those who wept their way through their stories. Then we shared in the joy as we heard the eventual victory that God gave to the humble repentant.

"For I say, through the grace given unto me, to every man that is among you, not to think of himself more highly than he ought to think; but to think soberly, according as God has dealt to every man the measure of faith." [176]

"Humble yourselves in the sight of the Lord,
and he shall lift you up." [177]

Job had a tough way to go in learning more about God's ways. He thought his righteousness and material possessions were rewards from God for his good living, instead of gifts of God's love. He did not have the gospel as we have it today, and could not know about commitment unto perfection, as we can. He learned that affliction opens one's eyes to disbelief and repentance for spiritual growth.

God lets us know if we fail under oppression and reveals what He expects of us. Sometimes we don't listen too well and needlessly indulge in "Poor Little Ole Me" (PLOM disease as we knew it in A.A.), until we get the message. Upon submission, God will show the reason and will heal through the Word.

The law of sin causes spiritual conviction. Walking in the Spirit gives assent to God's Word working in us. When we walk in the spirit, we are not walking in the appetites of the flesh. The two conditions cannot coexist in the Christian. Only through Christ can grace be received to walk in the Spirit. The Christian accepts the spiritual life and discards the flesh.

In the commitment unto perfection, the believer strives for complete sinlessness. The Christian who is not striving is not walking his commitment unto perfection. God reveals sin to the Christian and provides faith for grace to grow, when gratitude for grace is shown in Christian striving.

"If we say we have no sin, we deceive ourselves,
and the truth is not in us." [178]

Accepting sin in one's life is wrong.

*"If we say that we have fellowship with him, and walk
in darkness, we lie, and do not the truth. But if we walk in the
light, as he is in the light, we have fellowship one with another
("with the Father, and with his Son Jesus Christ") and the blood
of Jesus Christ his Son cleanseth us from all sin."* [179]

Hanging on to sovereignty of the believer and accepting sin in one's life, instead of humbly giving the sin to God, shows a poor attitude of complacency. The proper attitude in this case is illustrated by the parable of the Pharisee and the publican. The Pharisee prayed, in effect, "I thank God I am not a sinner like everyone else. I fast, pay tithes, etc."

Likewise, the Christian may pray, "Father, I thank you for Jesus and my salvation. I thank you because I am not condemned for sinning, because you have established my righteousness in Jesus Christ."

Praying this way without being sorry for the sin and not purposing repentance of that sin is displeasing to God.

Conviction may not be felt because of a seared conscience, and one may not feel spiritual pressure because the devil is happy about the situation, and a certain feeling of wellbeing may prevail. According to the Word, a Christian should feel uncomfortable if there is sin in his life.

The proper attitude is illustrated by the publican:

"God be merciful to me a sinner." [180]

Merely confessing sin is not walking in the Spirit. I religiously confessed sins for years and walked in the flesh to confess the same sins over and over until it became only a ritual. I am thankful to God for the freedom from ritualistic confession and the bondage of ignorance of His Word. I am thankful for the repentant confession He requires and has shown me. I am thankful that He mercifully grants grace for growth. I pray that I shall develop and maintain an attitude of true repentance until I hear His voice:

"Well done, good and faithful servant; thou hast been faithful over a few things, I will make thee ruler over many things; enter thou into the joy of the Lord." [181]

Am I perfect in the eyes of man? No.

Do I ever sin? Yes.

Do I accept sin in my life? No.

Do I feel condemned? No.

Do I feel conviction of sin? Yes.

Is God providing grace and removing the flesh? Yes.

Am I saved? Yes, through Jesus Christ and the power of His Resurrection!

Up to this point, *I* have done poorly in achieving spiritual perfection, but *God,* through the Holy Spirit, has done many wondrous works!

The reason so many Christians will not stand up and be counted is that they do not ask God to replace sin with the opposite fruit of the Spirit. In so living, they feel defeated because they are not overcomers. This leaves them open to condemnation by man, and feeling as if they had failed as a Christian, without a positive confession of possible perfection.

Many convictions about perfection are based on self-will and self-righteousness and are wrong. Practice of self-control or temperance is the individual choice in spiritual battles. I know, because I go through the routine of fighting self-will many times in my walk of striving, but I am not about to quit. The grace is available, and the winners develop a consciousness of this fact and overcome.

Going on to perfection means drawing closer to God and yielding to the Holy Spirit. To achieve perfection, one must constantly fight the battle against flesh, through application of the Word.

I have much to be thankful for, among which is the Atonement for my sins by the blood of Jesus Christ and security of eternal life through His Resurrection. I thumb my nose at the devil and pay my salvation premiums by striving in the Word of God (not with it), by running the race, through the blessings of His grace. Glory to Jesus Christ!

The law of sin prevails, but the power of sin has no hold on me.

"And when I saw him, I fell at his feet as dead.
And he laid his right hand upon me, saying unto me,
Fear not; I am the first and the last: I am he that liveth,
and was dead; and, behold, I am alive for evermore, Amen;

and have the keys of hell and death." [182]

From the response of unsaved people to sins that they see in a Christian's life (large or small), I detect a great number who reject Christianity because they think Christianity is about being perfect. They think a Christian should represent a perfect role model for all mankind. Striving for perfection is the in-process element of a Christian life.

Receiving Christ always brings liberation from sin and/or some other bondage but no one receives perfection or a gift of sinlessness.

It should be considered that even Jesus, who is and was perfectly sinless during His time on Earth, was often rejected for so many reasons.

We all want to meet the person who is perfect in thought, action, word and deed. That's why so many of us accept Jesus and look forward to seeing Him, face to face.

Chapter Five

Challenge

"Behold, now is the day of Salvation." [183]

WHY A SAVIOUR?

Salvation to many people, as it was to me, is just another word associated with religion. Being saved, in the minds of some, means being a "holy roller," who has fanatical ideas about things of God. That is pretty much how it was summed up for years by me.

I went through a series of hang-ups, including the one wherein I asked, "How can we be responsible for what someone did a long time ago?" or, "How could God be so cruel to send us to hell because we don't receive salvation, Christ, and are not what they call, saved?" The history of explanation is given in the first book of the Bible, Genesis:

"And the Lord God formed man of the dust of the ground,
and breathed into his nostrils the breath of life;
and man became a living soul.
And the Lord God planted a garden eastward in Eden;
and there he put the man whom he had formed." [184]

"And the Lord God commanded the man, saying, Of every tree
of the garden thou mayest freely eat: But of the tree of the
knowledge of good and evil, thou shalt not eat of it: for in the day
that thou eatest thereof thou shalt surely die." [185]

"And the Lord caused a deep sleep to fall upon Adam,
and he slept: and he took one of his ribs,

and closed up the flesh instead thereof;
And the rib, which the Lord God had taken from man,
made he woman, and brought her unto the man." [186]

The Garden of Eden was a garden of plenty. Adam and Eve were not as we are. Life would have been without sin and earthly death for all if they had been content to remain in obedient fellowship with God. In direct disobedience to God's command, they partook of the tree of knowledge, which enlightened their minds to good and evil. They hoped to be gods, as the devil, in the form of a serpent, convinced them that they would be. Instead, Adam and Eve caused death and condemnation of every generation. Only through Christ is the condemnation removed and eternal life with God made possible.

In case you ever wonder why you have to get up in the morning and go to work for a living, this is the reason. Yes, because Adam and Eve goofed—we all have to work for a living. This is what God decreed at the time, and it has been repeated down through the ages.

"In the sweat of thy face shalt thou eat bread till thou return
unto the ground." [187]

And for the ladies:

"Unto the woman, he said, I will greatly multiply
thy sorrow and thy conception, in sorrow thou shalt bring forth

children, and thy desire shall be to thy husband,
and he shall rule over thee." [188]

The Lord knows what each of us would do under the same circumstances. He created Adam and Eve and gave them free will, just as He has given free will to each of us. We are weak within ourselves. It has been proven many times over the centuries that no matter how much God will give, no matter how much mercy is extended, people are still going to falter and rebel against Him. We all know this is true. So what is the answer? That's right, salvation! God knew that, and He sent His only Son, Jesus, to provide that salvation.

Adam and Eve were created and put into a beautiful place to fellowship with God. Eve went against God's will and enticed Adam to do likewise. They exercised their free will and chose to go their own way, rather than stay in fellowship with God.

God placed instinct in mankind:

1. to know that there is a God;

2. to realize that He created the Earth, the universe, and all things.

"Because that which may be known of God is manifest in them;
for God hath shewed it unto them. For the invisible things of him
from the creation of the world are clearly seen,
being understood by the things that are made,
even his eternal power and Godhead;
so that they are without excuse." [189]

How often have we said, "There must be a better way." This is indicative of our instinct that there is a better way.

As a result of the fall of Adam and Eve, we have an inherent knowledge of right and wrong, which we wrestle with in our daily lives. We try to live by what we refer to as the things that are acceptable to society, a life standard for ourselves which we modify according to our desires, successes and failures. Unless we turn to God and His Word, we continue to seek gratification in material things and works of the flesh, and miss the reconciliation with God, forever.

Actually, we all get a shot at our own Garden of Eden by finding ourselves inherently in an attitude of pride and self-sufficiency. (Don't let this one go by; it happens to all of us). We are not condemned by those hereditary traits, but by our refusal to acknowledge that God is God and that we are not. For our choices we are responsible.

CONTINUED REBELLION

We don't have to look very far or think very hard to see that many lives characterize poor attitudes (unbelief), rebellion against God and His authority, or just negative indifference toward God and lack of love for fellow man. These things constitute sin.

I always considered myself to be a fair religionist, attended church regularly, went to Sunday School as a child, was raised in a strict religion, but was living a life of spiritual separation from God, as far as the true fellowship with Him was concerned.

People don't understand how they can be sinful. This is desire for self-will, independence from God's will, wanting to do their own thing. The world has managed to keep some semblance of decreasing stability while proudly running headlong toward many of the things that destroy instead of build.

In A.A., we looked at our lives and dug out all the areas of defect, as best we knew how, in order to survive. First of all, to be realistic, we needed to tabulate those defects for what they were, exclusive of the cause, or how they related to other people. Then we turned to God in obedience and diligent seeking of His will. This resulted in reaching out to help others.

I think of the alcoholic pit that God brought me from, the things He has done and the things He is doing now. It makes me enthusiastic about being a Christian, and my heart aches when I look at people who don't know what salvation is, don't know what it means to be saved. Some have accepted Christ and don't have much of an idea of what it is all about, because they do not read the Bible or spend time in prayer. Without the Word, one cannot set up a communication line through the spirit or cooperate with God's grace, which provides the faith for appropriation from Him.

The big factor is to learn to rely upon God for everything, instead of trying to run everything ourselves. I have lived in frustrating circumstances and repeatedly, have simply committed them to God, asked Him to work them out and show me what needs to be changed in me. After He showed me what needed to be changed, I yielded to Him in surrender, to the best of my ability, and have grown. God responds to all such situations if one does it in all sincerity, meekness, humility, love for Him and a true desire to do His will.

Without the understanding of the liberty in Christ and the power of the Resurrection, a person cannot help but live a self-centered, selfish, materialistic existence and have the same kind of a mind. The mind of a mature Christian is the mind of Christ, not the mind of an unbeliever.

"Now we have received, not the spirit of the world, but the Spirit which is of God that we might know the things that are freely given to us from God. But the natural man receiveth not the things of the Spirit of God for they are foolishness unto him, neither can he know them because they are spiritually discerned." [190]

Jesus, the crucified and resurrected Christ, released wisdom, the fullness of the Holy Spirit and power for us from God. This wisdom is not wisdom of the world, nor of evil spirits, but the wisdom of God in a mystery known only to God, and to Christians with a true experience. This wisdom that is hidden from Satan, even now is hidden from the minds of those who have not accepted Christ, who do not seek God through His Holy Word.

> *"But we speak the wisdom of God in a mystery,*
> *even the hidden wisdom, which God ordained before the world*
> *unto our glory: which none of the princes of this world knew:*
> *for had they known it, they would not have crucified*
> *the Lord of glory."* [191]

The world today is in bad shape and there are signs that we have never seen before that are alarming people. I'm not just talking about immorality; mankind has always been immoral. People are alarmed because of such things as world-wide over-population, disease, famine, atomic weapons, water pollution, shortages, gross failure and misdirection by world leaders, and a general loss of control in most areas of life.

Man tries to console himself by saying, "History repeats itself. We have seen all this before." But we have not seen all this before. Jesus said,

> *"Behold, I send you forth as sheep in the midst of wolves:*
> *be ye therefore wise as serpents, and harmless as doves."* [192]

He foretold of the false leadership that would prevail in government, in religious doctrines, and every other phase of life. He told of the greed, self-gratification, apostasy and hypo-critical stand that would prevail even among "His people," while hanging on to "sovereignty of the believer."

The gross proportions of immorality are the result of the insecurity of people trying to gratify and justify themselves in things of the flesh. The great feeling of insecurity that is sweeping the hearts of mankind today is the result of the lack of repentance and the lack of the Word of God in the heart. I have never seen so many people who are simply hungry for "something." Hearts are being oppressed by obvious fear, prevalent because of world conditions today. Out of the mouths of many come such statements as: What is the world coming to? There must be an answer! What are we going to do? Sad days are ahead for the little children of the world. Many of these calamities are not new, but the increase in number and severity are new and indicative of the closing end time.

God's Word and divine order are still being ignored by mankind and the world is reaping the results. God has a divine order:

1. God
2. Christ
3. Man
4. Woman
5. Children

"But I would have you know, that the head of every man is Christ; and the head of every woman is man; and the head of Christ is God." [193]

"Children, obey your parents in all things:
for this is well pleasing unto the Lord." [194]

Greed is padding the pocket, creating the desire for more gratification through material, worldly things; and is warping the minds of the world leaders, who are selling out their people. Countries are arming themselves with nuclear weapons in order to gain more power. Industry cares little about water pollution at a site where people picnic or go for a Sunday afternoon outing, as long as the dollar comes in and the public foots the bill for the pollution clean-up. The majority of people are scheming for future security in the dollar, while new methods are being devised every day to steal away that dollar. Man is rebelling against Jesus, and Satan is capitalizing on it. God is letting mankind have its own way, just as He permits practicing alcoholics to have theirs.

"For the wisdom of this world is foolishness with God:
for it is written, He taketh the wise in their own craftiness." [195]
"This wisdom descendeth not from above, but is earthly,
sensual, devilish." [196]

God's displeasure and call for repentance are synonymous throughout the Bible.

"I smote you with blasting and mildew
and with hail in all the labours of your hands:
yet ye turned not to me, saith the Lord." [197]

Likewise, Godly obedience and prosperity are synonymous.

> *"Blessed is the man that walketh not in the counsel*
> *of the ungodly, nor standeth in the way of sinners,*
> *nor sitteth in the seat of the scornful.*
> *But his delight is in the law of the Lord;*
> *and in his law doth he meditate day and night.*
> *And he shall be like a tree planted by the rivers of water,*
> *that bringeth forth his fruit in his season;*
> *his leaf also shall not wither;*
> *and whatsoever he doeth shall prosper."* [198]

The world keeps moving closer to the end time and is facing a coming tribulation, that people don't want to hear about.

Mankind in its liberalism is drifting further away from God, as people not only continue to reject Jesus and the Holy Bible but try to make sinful lifestyles acceptable. Satan is pouring out greater affliction upon all, including Christians, while God is pouring out His Spirit to encourage mankind to accept Christ and make a commitment, that more may be saved and that the Church will be free of spots and wrinkles.

Since man is remaining lukewarm to Christ, he is failing as the head of the house, in God's divine order. Likewise, women are not only continuing to rebel against God and man, but are taking an accelerated initiative, such as in the Women's Liberation Movement. As a result, children are also disregarding God's divine order by imitating their misguided parents. Many are embracing homosexuality, and divorce is fast approaching claim to every second marriage. The situation has reached serious proportions, as God tests man's free-will and challenges the hearts of all.

I believe the time has come for shocking experiences in the churches as well. The gospel is causing division and strife in the home and in the Church as the result of choice between repentance and commitment or disobedience and complacency.

"...There is no man that hath left house, or brethren, or sisters, or father or mother, or wife, or children, or lands, for my sake, and the gospel's, But he shall receive a hundredfold now in this time, houses, and brethren, and sisters, and mothers, and children, and lands, with persecutions: and in the world to come eternal life." [199]

"He that is not with me is against me; and he that gathereth not with me scattereth abroad." [200]

"Jesus sayeth unto him, I am the way, the truth, and the life: no man cometh unto the Father, but by me." [201]

"Have I been so long time with you, and yet hast thou not known me...?" [202]

"Sanctify them through thy truth: thy Word is truth." [203]

There must be an answer.

Those who want security, prosperity, and peace of mind will turn to Christ and the Word of God. Only Jesus can give these things through the Word and total trust in God. Searching in other places leads to continued frustration.

"Thou wilt keep him in perfect peace,
whose mind is stayed on thee: because he trusteth in thee." [204]

"Return unto thy rest, O my soul; for the Lord hath
dealt bountifully with thee." [205]

"To whom he said, 'This is the rest wherewith ye may cause
the weary to rest; and this is the refreshing;
yet they would not hear'." [206]
"Take my yoke upon you, and learn of me; for I am meek
and lowly in heart: and ye shall find rest unto your souls." [207]

"And having made peace through the blood of his cross,
by him to reconcile all things unto himself; by him, I say,
whether they be things in earth, or things in heaven." [208]

There is an answer! The answer is Jesus Christ, the only living God, as witnessed by many after His crucifixion and resurrection.

What are we going to do?

Some are going to make the decision to accept Christ, get into the Word and seek God until the peace comes. Others are going to recommit their lives to Christ and witness their way into the ministry of reconciliation until they become fruitful. Still others are going to increase their efforts to help more people find the peace they enjoy, in the walk of faith. Then there are those who will continue as they are, getting worse until they are lost or go into the tribulation.

"This know also, that in the last days perilous times shall come.
For men shall be lovers of their own selves, covetous, boasters,
proud, blasphemers, disobedient to parents, unthankful, unholy,
without natural affection, truce breakers, false accusers,
incontinent, fierce, despisers of those that are good, traitors,
heady, highminded, lovers of pleasures more than lovers of God;
Having a form of godliness, but denying the power thereof;
from such turn away." [209]

"Yea, and all that will live godly in Christ Jesus shall suffer
persecution. But evil men and seducers shall wax worse
and worse, deceiving and being deceived." [210]

Sober alcoholics have much to gain because of their repentance in the A.A. program. They have an advantage in having executed initial repentance and having been broken.

"Sorrow is better than laughter; for by the sadness
of the countenance the heart is made better." [211]

Sober alcoholics have the conviction of broken bondage and an open door to the liberty in Christ.

As one gains knowledge of the Word and refuses to repent, the hardening of the heart sets in, and the person loses his spiritual conscience or knowledge of himself. This is the beginning of apostasy.

"Ye therefore, beloved, seeing ye know these things beforehand,
beware lest ye also, being led away with the error of the wicked,
fall from your own steadfastness." [212]

God gave us His Word to live by so that we might benefit in growth, be broken and perfected. Until one is broken from the natural, sinful individuality in which he is born, he is still resisting God's grace and cannot serve God as one who is dedicated to the Word. Individuality, in self-image, serves self. Individuality, in humble unity with Christ, serves God.

As a practicing alcoholic, I repeatedly got drunk and then wallowed in remorse until I came to true repentance.

As a repentant Christian I am strengthened with a commitment through sanctification against backsliding into the sinful state of the "old man."

Renewing of the Mind

A renewed mind is a mind that has reached the place ordained by God in one's commitment unto perfection, dedication in loving sacrifice, striving for holiness according to God's grace, and turning away from worldliness to bear fruit in service to God. It is the mind of a person walking in the Spirit with the conviction that the life lived is acceptable and pleasing to God, knowing that trusting God is faith.

That ordained state is the place in which one is made subject to higher powers according to God's will. These higher powers refer to God and any and all authority God places above us. This again refers to His divine order, including civil authority, which He holds responsible, according to His Word.

"Let every soul be subject unto the higher powers.
For there is no power but of God: the powers that be are ordained
of God. Whosoever therefore resisteth the power, resisteth
the ordinance of God: and they that resist shall receive
to themselves damnation." [213]

Understanding God's will in this light, we can again readily see why the world is in such a state today. It's a result of rebellion against God in refusing to accept Christ or to walk in the Spirit. We can see the result of a world that is not committed to God and His Word.

The tricky part here is that much authority is becoming only positional, powerless, and unloving. What I mean is that the immorality and liberalism that is being exhibited by so many in positions of authority is turning people against authority, creating general lawlessness and causing mistrust and cynicism. Authority cannot command respect while talking out of both sides of the mouth. Many now are being called cynics because they speak the truth about those in authority and expect accountability to be a two-way street. It's okay to be truthful, but the difficulty for both sides lies in maintaining the truth in a spirit of love, without which one becomes critical.

The renewed mind acknowledges God in all things, discerning by the Word the difference between right and wrong and seeking those things pleasing to God, according to the Law of Love. It is the mind that desires to feed regularly on the Word and to be obedient to the Holy Spirit, moment by moment, knowing that God is leading; it is the mind that meditates on the Word, longing for more of divine revelation and the ways of God, utilizing the divine knowledge in striving for growth and fruitfulness, reaching for grace and turning away from temptations, in appreciation for grace.

Those who resist authority, resist God. It is the responsibility of each person to do good in all things in order to walk with a clear conscience of heart. The rebels walk in strife, as a result of disobedience to God.

"Wherefore ye must needs be subject, not only for wrath, but also for conscience sake." [214]

Those who submit to God's Will bear fruit of the Spirit by fulfilling the Law of Love. Moving away from the old ways and drawing closer to God, grace abounds and God is placed above all things.

The greatest pitfall in this area, which was revealed to me, is in judgment. The rebel claims justification through faith in Christ, just as those do who submit to God's Word in successive victories through striving for perfection.

God will judge all for their faith in Jesus Christ and by the works done. To have faith in Christ is to believe that He is the great Liberator who has provided the grace to be overcomers. Nothing can keep us from loving Christ in any tribulation, except our own will.

"Nay, in all these things we are more than conquerors through him that loved us." [215]

The rebel has never known the peace and comfort that God gives when one kneels, broken before Calvary, knowing this is the true justification, and that Jesus is the one who made it possible. Greater strides can be made on the spiritual knees than on the carnal feet.

"The sacrifices of God are a broken spirit: a broken and contrite heart. O God, thou will not despise." [216]

Therein is the rest, when all the burdens are put on Jesus, in complete admission of helplessness and spiritual poverty. Since I began kneeling at the foot of the cross, God has blessed me with more grace and more victories and let me know that this is the real justification. He gives grace to the one who comes to Him in this manner, because this is His will.

Jesus breaks every fetter, but not in the nakedness of adultery or fornication, with a murmured, "I'm sorry." God clearly forbids the works of the flesh.

> *"And that, knowing the time that now it is high time to*
> *awake out of sleep: for now is our salvation*
> *nearer than when we believed.*
> *The night is far spent, the day is at hand: let us therefore cast off*
> *the works of darkness, and let us put on the armour of light.*
> *Let us walk honestly, as in the day;*
> *not in rioting and drunkenness,*
> *not in chambering and wantonness, not in strife and envying.*
> *But put ye on the Lord Jesus Christ, and make not provision*
> *for the flesh, to fulfill the lusts thereof."* [217]

As God will judge by the Word, we are admonished to judge by the same Word. I have known some who claim liberty from the law to be justification for all the works of the flesh. Scriptures on liberty from the law have to do with only the following:

1. What we eat or drink

2. With whom we eat or drink

3. Where we eat

4. Where we buy food

5. Keeping the Sabbath

6. Circumcision

7. The law of Moses

8. What we wear and the keeping of customs

Each person disposes of these things according to the desire to please God.

"For the kingdom of God is not meat and drink; but righteousness, and peace, and joy in the Holy Ghost." [218]

Faith in Christ is not enjoying sin and saying, "That is why sin is beautiful, in a way, because we can only be righteous in Christ."

"What shall we say then? Is there unrighteousness with God? God forbid." [219]

God did not send His only begotten Son that we might continue in sin, and do so more abundantly in an attitude of complacency. Jesus said,

"Whosoever will come after me, let him deny himself, and take up his cross, and follow me." [220]

"For my yoke is easy, and my burden is light." [221]

Accepting Christ without going on to true repentance is rebellion and continuing in the old way. The reason for so much error in this area is self-will, contrary to the Word of God.

"For they that are such serve not our Lord Jesus Christ,
but their own belly; and by good words and fair speeches deceive
the hearts of the simple." [222]

God has mercy on those who repent. Those who refuse to repent become hardened through the deceitfulness of sin. Works of the submissive believer are the result of the Holy Spirit's direction, by the grace given, in appreciation for God's mercy, through the power of the Resurrection.

By God's grace, I want to be on the team that stands before Him as those who took up the cross and bear the marks of the cross on their bodies—those who took on the whole armor of God and fought the battles, losing some but winning more, by faith in Jesus. I want to be able to say,

"Father, I put my faith in Jesus to win them all; I am sorry that I didn't win them all, because of my weaknesses."

"There is therefore now no condemnation to them which are in
Christ Jesus, who walk not after the flesh, but after the Spirit." [223]

God forbid that I should be on the team that had not experienced the grace of God to overcome, through neglect of striving or lack of appreciation for the grace that Jesus made possible—those who latched onto justification and sought their liberty from the Word of God and interpreted grace as a catch-all for the works of the flesh. The rebel cannot understand the available grace until the true liberty in Christ is understood.

> *"But whoso looketh into the perfect law of liberty,*
> *and continueth therein, he being not a forgetful hearer,*
> *but a doer of the work, this man shall be blessed in his deed."* [224]

We know the mind is being renewed when we look back and see the difference in our lives, in agreement with God's Word; when we have spiritual conviction that we are moving with God's grace and are released from bondage, according to the liberty in Christ; when we find we are walking in faith and good works resulting in fruitfulness by the Spirit's guidance; and when we no longer seek the worldly things as we used to.

One of the most significant elements of the renewed mind is the new conscience that God gives, free of religious bondage and other inherited bondage. We do not renew our minds or conscience by works. God renews our minds when we surrender "self" control and shift to Christ control. The beginning of the renewal is the acceptance of Jesus Christ as our Saviour.

Faith concerns an attitude toward God, His Word, and submission to Him, in service.

"Whosoever therefore shall be ashamed of me and my words
in this adulterous and sinful generation;
of him also shall the Son
of man be ashamed, when he cometh
in the glory of his Father with the holy angels." [225]

The rebel is anyone who resists God's will, especially one who has the knowledge of the Word. The rebel is the one who has the Word by reading it, by anointed preaching, and sharing with other Christians, but who has set it aside, possibly under the heading of salvation by works. The entire Word of God is meant for all Christians to grow by and to be used as the guide for striving for perfection.

"All Scripture is given by inspiration of God, and is profitable
for doctrine, for reproof, for correction, for instruction
in righteousness: That the man of God may be perfect,
thoroughly furnished unto all good works." [226]

The proper attitude is an attitude of true sorrow, grief for having failed, a plea for more grace, thanksgiving for the grace already received, appreciation for the victories given through the grace and mercy from God, a desire to be closer to God, and the admission that it is not through works that grace comes but rather by exercise of the free will to obey God's Word as grace is provided. This is an attitude of humble nakedness before God and not the maintenance of pride, arrogation, and complacency.

Through Christ, the Christian has been sanctified. Sanctification is holiness and walking in a commitment to Christ. The test for basis of practical Christianity is consecration.

A prime fallacy, common to the rebel, is assuming that sanctification is automatic, with no participation by the person except to accept Christ. Accepting Christ without true repentance, without continued daily repentance, without consecration, striving, and a total commitment to Christ and all of God's Word is walking in the flesh, not in the Spirit. One who is walking in the Spirit has attained the proper place in commitment unto perfection and walks daily in humility before God, knowing freedom from condemnation, by the blood of Jesus Christ in the true sense.

Agreement to obey the Word of God is the secret to a healed and successful world.

"It is written, Man shall not live by bread alone,
but by every word that proceedeth out of the mouth of God." [227]

Disagreement to obey the Word of God is a cause of dissension and discord. The insignificant qualms of the liberty from law should not be disputed, but applied to one's life in such a way that it will not be a stumbling block to others.

The Lord is renewing my mind and giving me a new vision in life. It is the vision of a Christ-like mind, free of all the sin and uncleanness that once enslaved my thoughts and life: a vision of a mind that is humble before Calvary, in gratitude for the liberties that Christ provided; a mind that is at rest, with peace and quiet joy, in thanksgiving, and appreciation for the grace that abounds; a mind that knows God's will and is free from torment due to disobedience or rejection of God's will in any area, knowing that God is leading, simply by trusting Him; a mind that "knows in whom I believe," that expects miracles from a living God and knows the victory over the negative way, that knows the mercy and love of God and wants to see all people walk in that love; a mind that knows the truth and the way and the life.

The renewed mind is obtained by ready acceptance of and obedience to the Holy Spirit's call to repentance, prayer, and action, according to His guidance; and by making a commitment to Christ and walking that commitment, by the grace of God, to the best of one's ability.

The renewal of the mind begins with the exercise of faith. We exercise faith when we step forward to accept Christ, fear God, trust Him on the throne of our lives, pray for grace, search the Word in confirmation of the leading of the Holy Spirit and expect God to make Himself real to us. Faith means moving without seeing the end result.

Atheists, and those "learned" ones who try to figure it all out ahead of time, fail, but continue trying to discourage those who would exercise faith. They can never understand the Word, because the understanding is given by the Holy Spirit only to those who make the commitment and are under the blood and under subjection to the Word, which includes sanctification and a desire to inspire others to accept Christ.

The promises of the Word are for those who become the children of God. Many people procrastinate and nothing is accomplished until, in faith, action is taken on their part.

Each step of repentance along the way, brings new understanding of the Word. One begins to discern between the flesh and the spirit. It is like a change of lights, as one fluctuates in striving for the right way. When the flesh is practiced, the light is red; when the spirit is exercised, the light is green. A consciousness is developed where this fluctuation is noticed, as one seeks to walk in the spirit. Grace is provided. In an honest effort to grow, one's will decides if it will reach for it. There is no limit for the one who is honest in striving, for grace and God will show the way.

Being led by one's feelings is a hindrance but being led by the Word brings the victories and the proper resultant feelings, with the fruit.

"...The spirit indeed is willing, but the flesh is weak." [228]

Too often self is content to be saved, walk in the flesh, embrace sins of omission and disregard the impressions of the Holy Spirit that are aimed at repentance.

Another hindrance to a renewed mind is self-pity. The flesh is hard to bend and cries out, "Why do these things happen to me?" Remember, we must keep in mind that God will not go against His Word. In obeying the Holy Spirit, we are protected from the enemy's attacks and freed from bondage. As time passes and we see results, we begin to accept God's judgment over ours and appreciate what God is doing in us.

New paths must be cut away from the old ones in order to walk in the Spirit and in truth. The crust of the road to Calvary has been softened by the precious blood of Jesus, so that old ways may be changed and new ways may be established on the straight and narrow. The body must be brought into subjection through discipline. The mind is quick to cover for the flesh, but the Word is quicker. We must be alert for the input of the Holy Spirit, which always comes prior to the thoughts of the flesh. This takes a conscious effort in releasing our old self-image and constructing our true image.

Just before Jesus gave up His Spirit on the cross, He said,

"It is finished." [229]

and the curtain in the temple was torn in two.

"Jesus, when he had cried again with a loud voice,
yielded up the ghost. And, beyond, the veil of the temple
was rent in twain from the top to the bottom;
and the earth did quake, and the rocks rent." [230]

This was symbolic of Christ's opening the way between us and the throne of God. The curtain had separated us from the Holy of Holies, where only the high priests could go. By Christ's death on the cross, the barrier was removed, and direct access to God was made possible through the Word. No man or religion can stand between us and God, without hindering a first-hand experience with God. The only access to God is through the Word and Christ's Resurrection. Many times, before I came to have direct knowledge of the Word, I drew close to God and had peace, but always fell away because I could not stay close or continue on the right path without the Word.

Everyone needs a renewed mind in order to grow in the fruit that we all longed for before coming to Christ. We need a renewed mind in order to walk in faith, continue in repentance, have sins forgiven, have bondages removed and go on to perfection and peace, which occurs only in resting in Christ.

No one is exempt from the Word of God, and ignorance of the Word is no excuse for not keeping it. Judgment will include the sin of omission of not reading the Word of God. God is pleased with those who eat the Word as daily bread for growth in Christ and put it into practice.

One may think that spirituality begins by placing God into proper perspective when the conscious walk is begun, in seeking Him. No. Spirituality begins by getting ourselves into proper prospective with God through a renewed mind. One cannot stir up God within one's self, but one has to accept Christ into one's heart and life before any Godly spiritual stirring can take place.

For a time I thought that I was trying to give God credit for things that He had nothing to do with. I thought so because I had not accepted Christ before those events, and I felt that they happened because of my abilities or as a course of natural destiny. This took place because I did not realize that He works in all lives, even before a commitment is made. Now I know that these events resulted from God's love for me, as they do for all people, even while we are sinners. It is only after a commitment is made, in faith, that we see how it works. "Oh, now I see! God has always been—it's just that I was blind, but now I see."

PLAN OF SALVATION

The plan of salvation is given in a series of Scriptures, which leads one to the point of decision of accepting Christ, by personal invitation.

Christ is received by faith. You can accept Christ and become a Christian by engaging in a simple prayer said to the best of your ability in which you ask Jesus to come into your heart. In your own words express your feelings to Jesus. You don't have to say a fancy prayer or have any pre-cut words or set pattern. Salvation is a gift of God and the Lord knows your heart. If you sincerely ask Christ to be your Lord and Saviour, the Lord will accept that. You need ask only once and believe it is done.

Upon accepting Christ, continue to believe and expect God to work in your life. It may take some time before you get tuned in so that you can recognize it, but the Lord will start to work in your life immediately. When I say "some time," I am speaking about larger things that you definitely will recognize as God's work in your life. Leave no room for doubt or discouragement that Christ is in your heart. Your thoughts should not be about whether or not you have gone through the proper procedure to accept Him, or on anything else that would discourage your faith.

Look to God to give you grace, which will increase your faith and keep you in a state of expectation of bigger and better things. This is an area where many new Christians fall. They pray and feel that God does not have time to hear them. "If" He is real and "if" He is going to do anything, and "if" this thing called salvation is real...and so, God doesn't answer their prayer as quickly as they feel He should. They become discouraged, not realizing that what they are doing is giving into the evil forces.

As a new Christian, one has the power of the Resurrection, the power that God gives to live the abundant life, but the enemy tries to steal it away before its potential is realized. Thus the new Christian embarks on a path of spiritual warfare and must exercise faith.

God knows what we *need* and when we need it. We don't get everything we want, in our own way. God does give us things we want, but He is more concerned with what we need that will benefit us the most. When God gives, He gives big; so ask big.

When you pray, believe. Give God time to work, while you thank Him, and give Him time to talk to you. He wants to do some things in your life, but can do so only with your willingness. He may want you to yield something in your life so that He may change it. All things in God's plan for you are given because of Jesus Christ and what He did. So when all things are in God's will and He is not speaking to your heart to change your life in a specific area, all you need to do is petition Him in the name of Jesus and it will be done, in His own time. All of us need repair work in our lives. The door of repentance is always open. The way to make the fastest accomplishments is to heed God's Word, do what He wants, and let Him work. This is a twofold thing. God will do His part. The question is, will you?

"Whatsoever we ask, we receive,
because we keep His commandments." [231]

God knows what He wants done and how to accomplish it—we don't. All His works are for you—both the things that He wants to do for you and the things that you may ask of Him. A small amount of faith goes a long way.

A Christian must pray, believe and wait. God realizes new Christians generally have little patience and little faith, and He gives one the amount of grace needed for the amount of faith needed at the time, but one must wait upon the Lord. If one falls into the category where he feels Christianity doesn't work for him, then perhaps he has little patience in other things and his outlook may lean toward the negative side.

I sometimes subconsciously pray the old prayer, "Lord... Please grant me patience.... Right NOW!"

"Let patience have her perfect work, that ye may be perfect and entire, wanting nothing." [232]

We know some of the shortcomings in our lives and we need to acknowledge them. We need to become accustomed to listening to God and the guidance of the Holy Spirit. He has tried for years to impress upon our minds things which would bring us to the saving knowledge of Jesus Christ and the abundant life. We turn Him aside because we live in a rebellious state of mind. We need to open hearts and minds to accept Christ, and if necessary, write down the things that God impresses upon us as we walk the walk. We then need to pray about them and watch God work in our lives.

Don't expect Christianity to be a "gimme" existence. Expect it to be an abundant life wherein you learn to submit everything to God, yield to the Holy Spirit, and then begin to live a life in the fruit. If you turn the impressions away that God gives you and do not permit the Holy Spirit to work in your life, you will continue in frustration until you reach the point of surrender and consecration.

Surrender is one of the biggest parts of becoming a Christian, because, that way, one has to trust God. Only in surrender can growth follow. I have learned that this does not mean doing your thing. It is important that one realize that every person coming to Christ has always lived a life of self-will. In surrendering to God, it is important to recognize the need to stop the self-will, which is resistance to the Holy Spirit. Surrender is non-resistance to the Holy Spirit and obedience to Him.

Growing in the Lord and getting answers to prayers is not always an easy thing. Many times the blessings are received in giving and being ready to have God make personal changes.

Some of you will find that life in A.A. has prepared you for the walk, but you will also realize that there is much to be done in reaching the fullness that God has always intended for you. You will realize that having been freed from the bondage of alcohol and living a life of sobriety is not the best that can be hoped for.

In A.A., one's sobriety seems to be everything. In a sense, that is true, but God also wants you to be freed from death, sin, all afflictions of the enemy, and laws outside the Law of Love.

The enemy fights to keep you in as much bondage as possible, as he keeps talking to you:

"You're sober, and that's a lot better than what you used to be."

"So what if you have other sins? They're not important."

"It's okay if you take a few tranquilizers, if it helps you stay sober."

"So your sickness is not healing. Everyone has health problems, even ministers."

"So you have a few bad habits—you can't do anything about them anyway."

"If you trust Jesus, you'll lose your sobriety."

"Anything you do is all right, as long as you don't hurt anyone and you stay sober."

The enemy has lost round one. He doesn't want to lose them all. Stay in A.A., but accept Jesus Christ into your heart and on the throne of your life, and go on to total victory.

Some find it hard to believe that one can receive Christ in such a simple manner. On the other hand, after being a Christian for a while, the generosity of God is seen in the gift of salvation. It is hard to believe that people will not accept Christ in that simple step of faith.

The following are the generally accepted Scriptures of salvation: (Please read them slowly—this is the voice of God.)

"For all have sinned, and come short of the glory of God." [233]

"For the wages of sin is death; but the gift of God is eternal life
through Jesus Christ our Lord." [234]

"But God commendeth his love toward us, in that,
while we were yet sinners, Christ died for us." [235]

"For by grace are ye saved through faith;
and that not of yourselves: it is the gift of God." [236]

"For God so loved the world, that he gave his only begotten son,
that whosoever believeth in him should not perish,
but have everlasting life." [237]

"If we confess our sins, he is faithful and just to forgive us our
sins, and to cleanse us from all unrighteousness." [238]

"For I am persuaded, that neither death, nor life, nor angels,
nor principalities, nor powers, nor things present,
nor things to come, nor height, nor depth,
nor any other creature, shall be able to separate
us from the love of God, which is in Christ Jesus our Lord." [239]

"That if thou shalt confess with thy mouth the Lord Jesus, and shall believe in thine heart that God hath raised him from the dead, thou shalt be saved." [240]

"For he saith, I have heard thee in a time accepted, and in the day of salvation have I succoured thee: behold, now is the accepted time; now is the day of salvation." [241]

SENIOR SALVATION

In this section, I would like to address seniors with regard to accepting Jesus Christ as their personal Saviour.

In 1970, I professed Christ consciously at the age of forty-one. At the time of starting this book, I was forty-six years of age. Although I realize it has been in God's time, I regret that I did not find God's true concept earlier in life.

Today, in 1998, I know that I am going to live forever and I live my life from day to day with that conviction. That is not in the assurance that people who are living by the standards of the world may think of it, but rather in the true spiritual sense, looking beyond the earthly death. In the worldly sense, I believe it's more a matter of pushing death out of the way and thinking, "It can't or won't happen to me!"

I know I will have an earthly death unless the rapture should come before that time. I do not have the fear of death as I had in the past. God has made Himself real to me, and I have the firm belief that I will be with Jesus, eternally. It is a wonderful thought to live with every day and to look forward to. I am grateful to God that I have had the true experience and that I am enjoying a quiet joy in the adventure of fellowship with Christ.

You who are seniors can be saved immediately, if you will allow it to happen. No matter what your life has been, how you have lived it, or what age you are, you can receive salvation.

In accepting Christ into your heart, you are truly born again. When you accept Christ, in repentance, every sin you have ever committed in your life is forgiven and you are born into the kingdom of God.

"And their sins and iniquities will I remember no more." [242]

From this standpoint, a senior citizen is very fortunate. It is a comforting thought, in latter years, to know that all the sins of the past life are forgotten by God, that you have been born again, white as snow, cleansed by the blood of Jesus.

I have seen senior citizens accept Christ when they were so aged or ill that they could not walk. I once prayed for (with) an eighty-four-year-old lady, who was near death, in a coma in New Orleans. I told her that I knew she could hear me, that I had come to tell her about Jesus and to pray with her. I told her that if it was her desire, she could accept Christ as I prayed. I proceeded to pray, and when I mentioned the Name of Jesus, she would try to open her eyes and move her mouth, in an effort to speak. After I concluded, I proceeded to tell her that if the prayer had been her desire, she was now safely in the arms of Jesus. She heaved a large sigh. I felt spiritual conviction that this had been her desire, just as I did a few days later, when I received word of her death. When I get to heaven, I expect a lady to approach me and say, "I am the little lady you came to pray for in the hospital, when I could not pray for myself." I claimed her soul in faith and I know the mercy and kindness of God.

There is no telling, in your life as a Christian, what God will do for you, or what God will show you. You can be sure, though, that if you accept Christ as your Saviour, you will have a peaceful departure and an eternity with Him.

I have seen senior citizens who have not had the real experience. Their latter years are excruciating ones of fear, pain, and unhappiness. I have seen senior citizens who were so aged and decrepit in body that they could hardly maneuver, but their bodies quake with the joy of Christ's Resurrection and the glory that is ahead for them to share.

Loneliness is a common dilemma in latter years, and the enemy makes the most of the opportunity to oppress the lonely one. He torments the senior citizen with negative thoughts and doubts. Escape from the oppression is sought in the company of others, in reading, in watching TV, or in other media. The Christian finds everything needed in the Holy Bible for peace of mind and acceptance of an earthly death.

Many senior citizens are active in witnessing to other people and sharing in the joy of seeing them turn to Christ. There is as much for the senior citizen to do as there is for others.

"Those that be planted in the house of the Lord shall flourish in the courts of our God. They still bring forth fruit in old age; they shall be fat and flourishing." [243]

Anytime one turns energies to helping others, even when in need themselves, God blesses and brings peace of mind.

The senior citizen need not have remorse for lost time, for senior salvation is as precious to the Kingdom of Heaven as any other, and all heaven rejoices for every soul that is saved. Many people live their entire life without accepting Christ. One can enjoy fellowship with Christ, in this world as well as in the next.

Those who cannot read should have someone read the Bible to them daily, or should use records and tapes of Scriptures and anointed preaching. Reading or hearing the

Word in times of oppressing circumstances, will strengthen one's faith, remove the oppression, and promote proper feel-ings and attitudes.

Some can no longer attend functions for spiritual fellowship but can have the fullness of God in the treasures of His Word.

The Lord is divinely constant and has promised that He will never leave us. We must maintain a communication with Him, through the Word.

"I will not leave you comfortless, I will come to you." [244]

God manifests Himself through the Word, and strengthens the promise of fulfillment for the future.

"Wherein God, willing more abundantly to shew unto the heirs
of promise the immutability of his counsel,
confirmed it by an oath:
That by two immutable things,
in which it was impossible for God
to lie, we might have a strong consolation,
who have fled for refuge
to lay hold upon the hope set before us." [245]

CHALLENGE

Writing His book has been my commission, following the leading of the Holy Spirit, in sharing my experiences and inspirations. It has been another part of my adventure, in exceptional blessing, knowing that it is part of God's will for my life. I have been under a discipline, staying open to the Holy Spirit, in recording what He has brought.

Before I accepted Christ, there were many things that I did not know about God and His true concept. I have presented most of the major ones in this book, that those who have had a spiritual awakening might know some of what God has in store for them.

Every sober alcoholic is a fighter and a winner and is always looking for a challenge in helping others and in seeking growth and new victories. There is always a fearless drive to face that which is feared by many others, and there is a confidence that will always bring one out on top. If I'd had the knowledge that I have today, I would have gone to the aid of that sick alcoholic brother at 3:00 AM on a Sunday morning, armed with the strength of the Word rather than considering taking a .38 revolver into a race-riot torn neighborhood.

I challenge you to new levels of spiritual growth. There are freedoms to experience, through emotional and spiritual battles, which you have been prepared for. There are adventures to live in overcoming self and hindrances to the fullness in Christ. There is power to be obtained and used in overcoming evil harassment in the search for freedom from the bonds of materialism and other hang-ups. There are the gifts and the fruit of the Holy Spirit to be gained. I challenge you to test the Word of God, experience the true meaning of the Lord's Prayer, establish direct communication with the Lord, find your place in the eternal plan, capitalize on the outpouring of the Pentecostal experience and realize a renewed mind, in Christ. You are challenged to join the true Church, in man's heart, take your proper place in God's divine order and claim God's divine healings.

As a new Christian, or a Christian with a new hope, you can go on in your quest to help yourself and others with power that you have never realized before. You can have endless victories of a personal nature and of a charitable nature towards others. I challenge you to move to higher levels of Christ-experience in your walk, to renew your commitment to Him, to live the abundant life in His fullness and share a rich eternity with Him.

In this closing paragraph, I challenge those who have not accepted Jesus as their personal rock and foundation, as their Saviour and bridge of reconciliation to the Father. I pray that you will not procrastinate in accepting the challenge, this moment, in reciting the following prayer to salvation.

A Salvation Prayer

Father, I come to you, in the name of Jesus, having unrest, because of my human nature. I ask you to grant me eternal life, a gift through Jesus Christ, who died for me. I thank you, Father, for the grace you have given me, to see your great love for me and faith to believe in Jesus. I confess all my sins and ask you to forgive me and grant me grace, that I might repent daily. I thank you, Father, for cleansing me now of all my sins. By your Word, I know that nothing can separate me from your love in Jesus Christ, whom you have raised from the dead. I thank you, Father, for hearing my prayer and saving me. Jesus, I love you and ask you to come into my heart, take the throne of my life, grant me grace in a commitment unto perfection, lead me into a life style pleasing to you and help me to trust you in all things. AMEN.

APPENDIX

Dedication:

SCRIPTURE

1   I Cor. 6:20

Preface:

SCRIPTURE

2   Psalm 18:36

Chapter One:

SCRIPTURE

3   John 10:10
4   John 8:31, 32
5   Psalm 34:10
6   Psalm 34:6
7   John 10:10
8   II Tim 1:7
9   Psalm 139:9, 10
10   Gal. 6:7
11   Job 7:3, 4
12   Matt. 6:34
13   Phil. 3:13, 14
14   Zech.3:2
15   Jer. 15:16
16   Rom. 8:22, 23
17   Titus 2:11
18   Rom. 8:24
19   Rom. 10:17
20   I Peter 1:23
21   II John 9
22   Psalm 16:11
23   I Peter 3:15
24   Rom. 7:19

25   Rom. 7:24, 25
26   Rev. 22:17
27   I Peter 1:16

Chapter Two

SCRIPTURE

28   Matt. 7:7
29   John 16:3
30   Ephes. 4:23
31   Jonah 2:2
32   Matt. 3:2
33   Matt. 4:19
34   Matt. 16:18
35   Matt. 28:19, 20
36   John 7:37–39
37   Acts 17:27
38   I Cor. 2:12
39   I Cor. 14:21, 22
40   Matt. 28:2
41   Acts 9:4
42   Acts 2:17
43   II Chron. 20:12
44   II Cor. 3:5
45   Mark 9:23
46   Phil 4:13
47   Luke 17:19
48   Joshua 24:15
49   I Kings 18:21
50   Lam. 3:40
51   Eze. 18:31
52   Ezra 10:11
53   Jas 5:16
54   Matt. 6:10
55   Psalm 10:17

56	I Peter 5:6
57	Col. 3:13
58	Matt. 6:12
59	Matt. 5:23, 24
60	Prov. 28:13
61	Psalm 105:4
62	Mark 16:15
63	Rom. 2:21
64	II Tim. 1:7
65	II Cor. 12:9
66	Matt. 7:10
67	II Thes. 3:3
68	Matt. 28:18
69	John 14:12
70	Luke 10:17
71	Luke 10:19
72	Ephes. 6:17
73	Matt. 16:19
74	I Peter 2:24
75	Prov. 6:2
76	I John 4:4
77	II Peter 3:8
78	I Peter 1:18–21
79	Acts 1:7–9
80	Acts 2:1–4
81	2:17, 18
82	Acts 2:21
83	Eph. 5:27
84	I Thes. 4:16, 17
85	Rev. 9:6
86	Rev. 6:12, 13
87	Rev. 21:4

Chapter Three

SCRIPTURE

88	Phil. 3:14
89	Rom. 8:16

90	Gen. 19:14
91	Gen. 19:17
92	Gen. 19:24, 25
93	Gen. 19:26
94	Gen. 19:28
95	John 6:37
96	Psalm 23:4
97	Matt. 6:8
98	Luke 12:31
99	Jas 5:13–15
100	Acts 16:31
101	Mark 15:25
102	II Tim. 1:12
103	I Thes. 4:15–18
104	Mark 16:15–18
105	Gen. 18:14
106	Hos. 4:5
107	Matt. 28:18

Chapter Four

SCRIPTURE

108	II Tim. 4:7, 8
109	Prov. 3:5, 6
110	Rom. 10:3
111	Heb. 3:14
112	I Cor. 12:12
113	I Cor. 12:6–11
114	Neh. 8:10
115	Heb. 4:12
116	I John 5:20
117	Rom. 10:17
118	Hosea 4:6
119	II Chron. 7:14
120	I Cor. 9:24
121	James 5:16
122	II Cor. 12:9
123	Luke 22:19

124	Luke 22:20
125	Luke 22:42
126	Gen. 9:4
127	Acts 15:20
128	Prov. 16:9
129	Prov. 16:33
130	Ephes. 5:6
131	I Cor. 11:31
132	I Cor. 11:32
133	Rom. 8:28
134	Jas. 2:17–19
135	Prov. 2:6, 7
136	Gal. 5:5, 6
137	Prov. 3:5, 6
138	Mark 10:15
139	Luke 24:46–48
140	II Cor. 7:10
141	Acts 17:24
142	Heb. 3:13
143	II Chron. 7:14
144	Matt. 5:48
145	Phil. 3:12
146	Psalm 90:7
147	Matt. 6:9
148	Prov. 2:6
149	Matt. 6:5, 6
150	Matt. 6:7, 8
151	Matt. 6:9–13
152	Rev. 3:20
153	Luke 17:10
154	Rev. 4:11
155	Job 42:2
156	Rom. 7:24, 25
157	Psalms 50:14
158	Phil. 4:6
159	I John 5:14, 15
160	Jas. 5:16
161	Matt. 6:14, 15
162	II Chron. 7:14
163	I John 4:10–12
164	I John 3:22, 23
165	John 15:7
166	Jas. 4:3
167	Mark 11:24
168	Rom. 12:1, 2
169	Ephes. 5:9
170	Gal. 5:22, 23
171	Gal. 5:19–21
172	Matt. 7:17
173	Jas. 4:17
174	Psalm 34:9, 10
175	Matt. 18:4
176	Rom. 12:3
177	Jas. 4:10
178	I John 1:8
179	I John 1:6, 7
180	Luke 18:13
181	Matt. 25:23
182	Rev. 1:17, 18

Chapter Five

SCRIPTURE

183	II Cor. 6:2
184	Gen. 2:7, 8
185	Gen. 2:16, 17
186	Gen. 2:21, 22
187	Gen. 3:19
188	Gen. 3:16
189	Rom. 1:19, 20
190	I Cor. 2:12, 14
191	I Cor. 2:7, 8
192	Matt.10:16
193	I Cor. 11:3
194	Col. 3:20
195	I Cor. 3:19
196	Jas. 3:15

197	Haggai 2:17	237	John 3:16
198	Psalms 1:1–3	238	I John 1:9
199	Mark 10:29, 30	239	Rom. 3:38, 39
200	Matt. 12:30	240	Rom. 10:9
201	John 14:6	241	II Cor. 6:2
202	John 14:9	242	Heb. 10:17
203	John 17:17	243	Psalm 92:13, 14
204	Isaiah 26:3	244	John 14:18
205	Psalms 116:7	245	Heb. 6:17, 18
206	Isaiah 28:12		
207	Matt. 11:29		
208	Col. 1:20		
209	II Tim. 3:1–5		
210	II Tim 3:12, 13		
211	Eccles. 7:3		
212	II Peter 3:17		
213	Rom. 13:1, 2		
214	Rom. 13:5		
215	Rom. 8:37		
216	Psalms 51:17		
217	Rom. 13:11–14		
218	Rom. 14:17		
219	Rom. 9:14		
220	Mark 8:34		
221	Matt. 11:30		
222	Rom. 16:18		
223	Rom. 8:1		
224	Jas. 1:25		
225	Mark 8:38		
226	II Tim. 3:16, 17		
227	Matt. 4:4		
228	Matt. 26:41		
229	John 19:30		
230	Matt. 27:50, 51		
231	I John 3:22		
232	Jas 1:4		
233	Rom. 3:23		
234	Rom. 6:23		
235	Rom. 5:8		
236	Ephes. 2:8		

Select Bibliography

This bibliography is not a complete record of all the works and sources I have consulted, as most of the information was lost in a fire, the details of which you will find in Chapter Three, "Fiery Exchange."

Alcoholics Anonymous World Services. *Alcoholics Anonymous.* 3rd edition new and revised. New York: Alcoholics Anonymous World Services, 1976.

American Bible Society. *Good News Bible – The Bible in Today's English Version.* New York: American Bible Society, 1976.

Bright, Bill. *Four Spiritual Laws.* Orlando: New Life Publications, 1994.

Bonhoeffer, Dietrich. *Life Together (Gemeinsames Leben).* New York: Harper & Row Publishers, Inc., 1954.

Chambers, Oswald. *My Utmost for His Highest.* Uhrichsville, Ohio: Barbour and Company, Inc.

Crank, David. *Freedom From Fear, Anxiety and Panic Attacks.* Tulsa: Harrison House, 1995.

Dake, Finis Jennings. *Dake's Annotated Reference Bible.* Lawrenceville, Ga.: Dake Bible Sales, Inc., 1978.

Douglas, J. D., M.A., B.D., S.T.M., Ph.D. *The New Bible Dictionary,.* Grand Rapids: Wm. B. Eerdmans Publishing Co., 1978.

Freeman, Dr. Hobart E., Th.D. *Biblical Thinking & Confession.* Warsaw, Ind.: Faith Ministries & Publications.

———. *Every Wind of Doctrine.* Warsaw, Ind.: Faith Ministries & Publications, 1974.

———. *How To Know God's Will For Your Life and For Important Decisions.* Warsaw, Ind.: Faith Ministries & Publications.

———. *Why Speak in Tongues?* Warsaw, Ind.: Faith Ministries & Publications.

Grubb, Norman. *Rees Howells Intercessor.* Fort Washington, Penn.: Christian Literature Crusade, 1993.

Hagin, Kenneth E.. *Healing Belongs To Us.* Tulsa: Kenneth Hagin Ministries, 1996.

Hagin, Kenneth Jr. *Healing Forever Settled.* Tulsa: Kenneth Hagin Ministries, 1989.

Harris, Thomas A., M.D. *I'm OK – You're OK.* New York: Avon Publishers, 1973.

Hazelden. *Twenty-Four Hours a Day.* Center City, Minn.: Hazelden, 1985.

Hemfelt, Robert, M.D., Minirth, Frank M.D., Meier, Paul M.D. *Love is a Choice*. Nashville: Thomas Nelson Publishers, 1989.

Johnson, Vernon E. *I'll Quit Tomorrow*. New York: Harper & Row Publishers, 1973.

Lindsay, Hal. *The Late Great Planet Earth*. Grand Rapids, Mich.: Zondervan Publishing House, 1970.

Milam, James R., Ph.D. *The Emergent Comprehensive Concept of Alcoholism*. Kirkland, Wash.: Alcoholism Center Associates, Inc. Press, 1978.

Miller, J. Keith. *A Hunger For Healing*. New York: HarperCollins Publishers, 1991.

Narramore, Bruce. *You're Someone Special*. Grand Rapids, Mich.: Zondervan Publishing House, 1978.

Presnall, Lewis F. *Search for Serenity*. Salt Lake City: Utah Alcoholism Foundation, 1959.

Satinover, Jeffrey, M.D. *Homosexuality And The Politics of Truth*. Grand Rapids: Baker Books, 1996.

Strong, James, S.T.D., LL.D. *The Exhaustive Concordance of The Bible*. Nashville: Abingdon, 1977.

Thompson, Frank Charles, D.D., Ph.D. *The Thompson Chain-Reference Bible*. Indianapolis: B.B. Kirkbridge Bible Co., Inc., 1964

Tozer, Aiden Wilson. *The Best of A. W. Tozer – Volume 2*. Grand Rapids, Mich.: Baker Books, 1995.

Wigglesworth, Smith. *The Complete Collection of His Life Teachings*. Tulsa: Albury Publishing, 1996.

Wilkerson, David. *The Vision*. New York: Pyramid Books, 1974.

ORDER FORM

Please send me _____ copy(ies) of *Sobriety AMEN*

Price U.S.A. (each): $14.95

Price Canada: $18.95

Postage (per book): $1.50

Tax (Arizona residents only): $1.05

Total: $ _____

Name _____

Address _____

City/State/Zip _____

Telephone _____

Mail orders to:

Providence Two

P.O. Box 2211

Chino Valley, AZ 86323